I0111397

To purchase *Tax Lien Certificates* go to the website
bakerinternational.org

Copyright © 2015 Baker International Publishing LLC

All rights reserved. No part of this book may be reproduced in whole or in part without written permission from the Copyright owner, except by reviewers who may quote brief excerpts in connection with review in a newspaper, TV, magazine, or electronic publication: nor may any part of this book be reproduced, stored in a retrieval system, or transmitted in any form or by any means electronic, mechanical, photocopying, recording, or other, without written permission from the Copyright owner.

ISBN-978-0-692-78907-0

Contact Us
Website - bakerinternational.org
E-mail - bakerinternational1@gmail.com
For Cover designs contact us via email

Printed in the USA

Table of Contents

Acknowledgements

First and foremost, I would like to thank God for giving me life, blessing me throughout my life, and giving me the ability to commence and complete this book. Next, I wish to thank my grandmother, Mary Davis for nurturing me as a child, loving me, and accepting me for who I am. To my parents, Henry and Esther Baker, thank you for bringing me into this world. Dad, may God continue to bless your soul; thank you for instilling in me manners, dedication, and discipline towards education, which is a trait I have passed down to my kids. Mom you have been so significant in my life. Thank you for being there for my mistakes, my triumphs, my adversity, and my rebirth. Thank you for showing me how to be an effective parent, as well as teaching me to have a relentless work ethic. No matter the circumstances you always kept the Baker family intact. For that I just want to say I love you and I'm honored to call you my mother.

I give special accolades to the one and only, my wife, Taeshawn Snow. Thank you for your unconditional love, endless support, unyielding loyalty, and your convictions that made me into the great man that I am today. I don't know where I would be without you. But what I do know is where my heart is, and it's with you forever. I would like to give special thanks to Sharmon Howell and the entire Howell and Wade family. Thank you for inspiring me to write this book, thank you for taking the time to help me get this book completed, thank you for the critique, the constructive criticism, the positive advice, the endless business dialogues we discussed for the future, and thanks for just keeping me balanced when I would sometimes deviate from the prize. Sharmon you are a business genius. Enjoy the success of your book and the fruitful profits from your endeavors.

A special thanks to Baker International Publising, thanks for giving me the opportunity to inform the masses about this best kept secret. Thank you for giving me the opportunity and allowing me the liberty to publish my own book, start my own book publishing company, and for assisting me with putting Baker International on the map. Thank you for the precise editing, the phenomenal book cover, and thanks for the preparation of the book. I would like to say thanks to Not Just Books store in Trenton, NJ for supplying me with books, and having in stock what I needed to do my research. Your assistance is very much appreciated.

I would like to give special thanks to these people: Darryl Henry, Jamal McCray, Omar Council, Myonoway Phelps, Brandon English, Stanley Narcisse, My mentor Patrick Crowe, Norman Parada, John Cooley, Akbar Pray, Mark Foster, Eric Flowers, (R . I . P) Todd Carter, Donald Welch, Julius Monyoukaye, Thaddeous Mcnair, Jason Rogers, Shawn Riley, and Kellen Dingmon.

I would like to give an extreme reference to my grandfather, James K. Baker who came into my life and simply taught me that life was about praying as a family, eating at the table as a family, studying together, having fun together, and ultimately, loving each other. You taught me the role a father/grandfather should play. All of those things stuck with me and my siblings. You will be missed forever. Rest In Peace.

I want to thank my family and loved ones here in America and in Liberia for uplifting me throughout the course of my entire life. You know who you are. God bless Liberia, America, and the entire world. I would like to thank the entire 682 M.L.K Blvd. for enabling me and embedding in me how to be a proprietor instead of an employee or consumer. Overall, thank you for allowing me the freedom to be unbossed (self-employed).

Finally, to my beloved children, James, Sundasia, and RaeVon Baker – I'm doing this for you guys. This is the beginning of the legacy I'm leaving behind for you all. You all encouraged me every day to complete this book. Without your support, I wouldn't have been able to bring this project to fruition. You guys are my number one supporters, and now that the book is completed you all deserve the credit. Thanks to each one of you and your support, Dad is now officially an author. Now we can put this on my list of accomplishments. James thank you for succeeding in life and becoming independent, brilliant, charismatic, and for being a mature young man when the odds were stacked against you. Sundasia, thank you for being a devoted scholar, moralist, classy young lady, and the athletic track superstar that you are. Continue to work hard because all your dreams are about to come true. I'm very proud of you. RaeVon, I want to thank you for being a great son. You are a

well-mannered respectful young man, and highly intelligent. The achievements you will accomplish in the future will be unprecedented. I can already see that you are prepared for your future success. My three wonderful children, I love you all equally with all my heart. May your talents take you to the Zenith unimaginable.

Introduction

One day I was reading the Barron's, a periodical about stocks and other investments. As I was turning the pages, I noticed that some companies were rising and some were falling.

After being overwhelmed with the ups and downs in the stock market that day, I had an epiphany. None of these investments, were safe. So I put the newspaper down and started reading an investment book called *Mutual Funds for Dummies*. The further I got into book, the more I really did feel like a dummy.

I felt like an idiot because I was dumb enough to buy the book. It was, as Yogi Berra once said "Like déjà vu all over again." Most of the books on the subject were referred to me by friends and associates, but it was the same old songs being played repeatedly. No matter how much I searched, I couldn't find an investment book that could tell me about a safe and secure reservoir with a high yield interest rate that was worth my time. I told myself "I'm not going to continue to overload my brain with this redundant information." That's when I did an analysis on the Barron's newspaper and the Mutual Funds book I was reading. I came to the conclusion that some companies were making money while some were losing money. Overall, these companies were all taking a big risk.

One thing I am not going do is gamble or take risks with money. All the investment books I had read only offered me ways to take risks with my own money, or were filled with unnecessary trivial information. I suddenly regretted wasting my money on those books.

In my 2009 Real Estate class, we learned about liens, foreclosure, and redemption. I noticed that when the teacher taught those topics he never mentioned that the tax liens investment was the safest and best investment since sliced bread. He may not have known or maybe he just didn't want to give the class some information that would make us wealthy. It was while reading *Principles and Practices of New Jersey Real Estate* that I was able to put two and two together. Specifically, page 294 of Chapter 15 invigorated me as I saw just how great an investment these Tax Liens were. Once I read that this sort of investment would allow me to earn an 18% interest rate, and I could also become a potential homeowner, I was very excited.

My real estate book didn't go into depth about this particular investment being safe. So I did my own research on Tax Lien Certificates. I had finally found an investment that was extremely safe and secure. As I finished my research on this investment, I realized this information had changed my life.

Now I no longer have to read redundant investment literature, get extremely painful headaches, or waste any more money.

I know you're probably saying to yourself, "what is going to make this guy's book distinct from any other investment books that have been written?" My answer, I'm going to give you one hundred percent actual facts that will allow you to make lucrative profits. Second it's a safe investment backed by real estate.

Now I know you are thinking this will be complicated.

Guess what? It's very simple and you don't need years of college or a vast amount of money to do it effectively. You will no longer need to keep investing your money in banks, credit unions, or any other financial institutions that have been depriving you of success. This safe investment is called, *Tax Lien Certificates.*

To learn all about this investment, all you have to do is continue reading on. I will dissect for you in the simplest form everything you need to know about tax lien certificates, including all the states that I have researched that are applicable for anyone to invest and make large profits. I was very passionate about making sure all the information wrote in this book is one hundred percent factual. And by the grace of God, I was able to achieve that.

Once you finish reading this book, it is my hope that you will be empowered and motivated to put all this valuable information to use to build your wealth or continue building your wealth.

Reading this book, you will see that each state and municipality vary in laws, interest rates, and the way they do business. So study the state or states in which you have the most interest. All of the state's offer safe investments along with high interest rates. I made this book simple for you without complications. I go into precise detail because I am adamant about being uncompromising when it comes to facts.

I also did you a great favor, by saving you the time, expense, and from reading unnecessary business books that will never tell you about great investments that are lucrative and safe. They will discuss investments that are mediocre and hazardous.

Take advantage of this opportunity. Why continue to gamble with your money by putting it in investment funds, or continue to get taken advantage of by financial institutions when you can change your life just by applying these simple guaranteed steps.

Work smarter, not harder!

Nyene Baker

Chapter 1
Is The Road to Being Successful Complicated?

If you keep your pockets full of coins, you will always have small change. – Yoruba Proverb

A lot of people sit back and contemplate ways to become affluent. During our lifetime we have come across or seen numerous schematic endeavors claiming to make us successful. Finally, I have what you've been waiting for. It's a safe investment people in America love to keep to themselves and it is called Tax Lien Certificates.

In this book I will give you the step-by-step process demonstrating how to profit from this investment. Don't get me wrong, I know it sounds inconceivable, but all the information in this book is factual and you will be able to verify these facts at your county or state offices.

I know you are wondering if this method is so safe why am I sharing it with the world and not keeping it to myself. My response is that your success does not take anything away from me. The more wealth I help others acquire, the more blessings I receive.

In this book you will notice that depending on which state you are in, you can make more than 24% interest per year on your investment, which is a total win/win situation. I know right now you are feeling dubious and you have the right to, but before you finish this quest for success you will be astounded by the information revealed in this investment book. I can assure you that you will consider it as one of the best you've read in your entire life.

I will give you the information you need to call your local government entity based on the state you live in. The first thing I want you to truly comprehend is that this investment called Tax Lien Certificates is very distinctive.

The reason I say this is because if you were to get consultation from a stockbrokerage firm, real estate firm, a banker at a bank or from any professional from a financial institution, none would be able to guarantee that their institution could assure you of a low risk investment with at least an 18% interest rate per year on your investment.

If you don't believe it, I encourage you to try to find the results. Once you find out what I said is true about those financial institutions not being able to offer you low risk, safe investments, you will fall in love with Tax Lien Certificates.

Once you call and verify the information I present, you will be ready to embrace this investment called Tax Lien Certificates. I have taken a great amount of time to provide you with this accurate information. This book is actually a guide for a safe investment. You have control at all times of your investment, so you don't have to worry about bankruptcies, fraudulent scams, or other people making a commission off you or your interest rate ever fluctuating. This investment is backed by real estate and approved by the government.

I was introduced to Tax Lien Certificates in 2009. At the time, I was a student at Princeton Real Estate School. While doing some homework, I was reading Chapter 15 of *Principles and Practices of New Jersey Real Estate,* written by Frank W. Kovats, Dre. This particular chapter focuses on liens, foreclosure, and redemptions. As I read page 295, I thought to myself, this is very interesting. After I finished the chapter, I contemplated that night about the information I'd just learned.

I was anxious to get back to class to ask the teacher about the information I'd read. Two days later, I made sure I got to class early so I could ask the teacher to explain precisely what I'd read.

The teacher explained it to me, but he explained it to me just like the book did, which was from an employee's perspective and not from an investor's perspective. I noticed that he was reluctant to let me know that I had struck gold. He tried to persuade me to focus more on being a real estate agent than on tax liens.

Once he said that; I realized he either knew about this successful investment being beneficial and didn't want me to benefit from it, or he was just a nincompoop. As I started to do more research on Tax Lien Certificates; I couldn't help but think to myself, *I must have been stuck in a coma all my life.* How is it I missed out on this enormous opportunity all my life? I realized where I went wrong. I wasn't around the right people, places, or in the right career to have known this information.

So what I started doing was befriending businessmen and women from all walks of life, your average 9-to-5 employees such as teachers, and even physicians. I would start a conversation with them, and then out of nowhere I would ask if they had ever heard about Tax Lien Certificates?

If they said they knew about Tax lien Certificates, I'd then pretend to know nothing about the subject to see if they really knew what they were talking about.

I kid you not, most people had never heard of Tax Lien Certificates. Then you had some that had heard about them and tried to explain it to me, but really couldn't because they didn't have an inkling about this investment strategy. There were also a few who knew a little about them, but provided a lot of wrong information for the most part. Some even confirmed that they used to invest in them yet they really couldn't depict to me what they were all about. Finally, I conversed with a few who really knew about them; however, even some of them still didn't really have all their facts in line.

And since I was asking doctors, teachers, other college students, professional people, and others, I was flabbergasted as to how so few were educated on Tax Lien Certificates. Two days into doing my survey, I didn't feel so bad after all about being thirty years old and oblivious to the subject.

I finally had an epiphany on why my real estate teacher told me to focus more on being a real estate agent than on Tax Liens. As I kept doing my research, I ran into a few real estate agents and brokers who also had no clue about Tax Lien Certificates. It was then that I understood why my Real Estate teacher said to me that real estate agents and brokers don't sell Tax Lien Certificates with their license, they can only sell properties. They can't sell Tax Lien Certificates and earn a commission, they can only get commission for selling properties.

It was obvious that because they can't make a dime from Tax Lien Certificates, they don't care to know about them. Little did my teacher know, I had bigger plans than only becoming a real estate agent. My actual intentions were to become more informed about real estate in order to become a real estate investor.

I believe my teacher knew Tax Lien Certificates were a lucrative business, but just like the majority of Americans who know about great opportunities, he too wanted to keep that secret to himself.

Years ago I use to always hear people talk about how you could go to the court house in Trenton, NJ on South Broad St. to participate in property auctions. I would also hear how one could go to City Hall in downtown Trenton to get a list of tax liens, but I had no clue what tax liens were, nor did I know the purpose of the auctions, so I never inquired.

I also heard there was an advertisement regarding these tax lien auctions in the paper listed yearly, but I didn't have an inkling as to when exactly it was posted in the newspaper. Yet, if I had stumbled across the advertisement at that time, I wouldn't have even made an attempt to attend the auction anyway. I was uninformed and oblivious to real estate. Even though I wasn't looking for the advertisements of the auctions it was passing me by every year. I'm sure I'm not the only person who wasn't paying attention, so I don't feel bad. Well now it's 2014 and besides Tax Lien Certificates, I still haven't run into an investment that is safer than this.

Today is September 20, 2014. Alibaba, a company in China made history. It was the highest Initial Public offering in stock market history. An I.P.O. is the first sale of stock by a private company to the public. The price reached $90.28 per share, and the company made a vast amount of money. People that invested in Alibaba made a lot of money, but since the stock market moves are often based on emotions they are winners today but could be losers tomorrow.

It's safer to invest in Tax Lien Certificates than to invest all of your 401k in stock of the company your work for. If you invest all of your 401k in your company's stock, you'll lose everything if the company's stock plummets and goes bankrupt. With Tax Lien Certificates you don't need to hire financial advisors or financial planners and waste money paying them for nothing. It's so simple you are always in control. Always remember the interest rate is guaranteed by whichever branch of government is issuing the Tax Lien Certificates, and they are secured by real estate.

Chapter 2
Please Enlighten Me On What A Tax Lien Certificate Is?

You must never be stupid enough to say or smart enough to admit you know what someone else is talking about. The moment you do your learning stops. –Awo Osun Kunle

The history of land ownership explains how tax liens came about. The government taxed property owners for their purchase of land; which is a benefit, yet the catch was the owner had to pay taxes on the property they bought. These taxes were a significant source of funding for government agencies and continue to be so today. Taxes are used to pay for a wide variety of governmental services and programs including national defense, social security, fire and police protection, road construction, city maintenance and our educational systems.

Due to adversity or whatever issues taxpayers may have if they are not able to pay their annual taxes on time, their property goes into default. In the early 1800s local governments devised a plan that would help avoid taking massive financial loses when people didn't pay their taxes. They came up with a rate of interest to be imposed on the property owner who was not prompt with his tax payments. The intention of this penalty was to encourage people to pay on time. The taxes and penalty imposed, formed a lien on the property. The penalty for not paying one's taxes incurred interest rates that ranged from as low as 6% on up to more than 25%. One could also even accumulate more than that.

Due to tax lien debts and liens on properties, local governments from various states started what we now call, Tax Lien Certificates. Since the local government needed its money expeditiously, the certificates served as a means to ensure that they would still be paid. This occurred once the tax lien placed on one's property was paid. As a result of the debt being satisfied, the certificate was then given to the investor. Once the investors purchased the Tax Lien Certificates, they were bound to the same penalties and taxes to which the previous owners were bound. All of the local entities received their money instantly from investors. The investors were free from any worries because they were in a similar position as the government; therefore, they had the same rights to the taxes and penalties. So, if taxpayers neglected to pay their taxes, the government had the right to foreclose on and seize their property.

Tax Lien Certificates gave investors the same entitlement. After a certain time if the property owner didn't pay his taxes the investor could acquire the title to the property. This particular government program has been so successful that over 40% of the states have laws that allow counties and other taxing constituents to sell Tax Lien Certificates to investors.

To be abreast of Tax Lien Certificates one should be conscious of real estate laws and principles, especially tax lien laws. Now some of you are already educated on tax liens, so let me commend you. Yet, for those who don't know what a lien is, it is a right given by law to a creditor to have a debt or charge satisfied out of the property belonging to the debtor. Liens on property may be either voluntary, arising from an act of the owner such as the execution of a mortgage or they may be involuntary and created by operation of law such as tax liens or judgement liens recorded by the creditor of the owner.

Involuntary liens do not require the owner's consent. A property lien is a hold or claim which one person has upon the property of another as security for a debt. All liens are recorded in the county the property is in, and it is also public information. Since this is public information, one can go to any City Hall or county courthouse, depending on which state they are in to check on liens that are on any inch of land or property in America.

The older the liens are, the more priority they are given over the newer liens. All liens are not equal. For example, if the property has a lien that is placed on it, the first lien is entitled to have the rights to that property, the second lien is entitled to the rights to the property prior to the rights of the first lien.

Let me give you an example. Say you buy a house and obtain a mortgage or trust deed, from a lender these are the forms of liens. The lender will imply that this lien be the (primary) lien to protect the loan. Now say years later you borrow money using the equity in your house as security, it will (cause) an additional lien to be placed on that property. It would be second in place to the original mortgage or trust deed. If the original mortgage holder decides to foreclose on the property, it will alienate all other liens, and the original lien holder will gain sole possession of the property. It will also be free and clear of all other liens. This is imperative, so take note.

A tax lien is superior to all other liens except IRS liens and a majority of state liens. If a tax lien is filed against a property owner, under no circumstances will they be able to sell, trade, or discard of the property without this particular lien being paid.

A property tax becomes a lien when a property owner fails to pay their taxes when due. This lien is superior to the first mortgage or the first trust deed. Should the county be forced to foreclose, all lesser liens will be erased. Property owners' mortgage lenders establish an escrow account in which part of their monthly payment is deposited. This is done for the purpose of having funds available to pay taxes when due. The lender uses the money in the escrow account to pay the taxes.

The county and state where the property is located will provide all the provisions of a Tax Lien Certificate. The owner of the certificate doesn't have communication with the owner of the actual property. The county collects the tax money from the property owner. This also includes any accrued interest or penalties that the property owner owes. The county then sends all of the collected money to the Tax Lien Certificate owner.

You won't have to devote all of your time just to become skilled in this profession. Once you read this book thoroughly you will learn everything you need to know about Tax Lien Certificates. Now, one thing about Tax Lien Certificates they are a very assuring investment while stocks, bonds, and mutual funds are all high risk investments. They don't offer a safe stability like Tax Lien Certificates.

As I said before, the interest rates vary from state to state. Tax Lien Certificates are governed by law, so one never has to worry about interest rates declining.

Once you do your due diligence, you will already be informed about the interest rates in the state that you choose. The thing about Tax Lien Certificates is you can buy many of them. There is no particular limit, but to be sure, check with City Hall or County Courthouse within the state you are interested in.

Many of the elite companies spend an enormous amount of money on Tax Lien Certificates and reap large profits in return. If you put your mind to it, you can create one of these companies and be very successful.

Iowa and some parts of Maryland have a 24% interest rate. Now, that is great news for people who live in these states or who have plans to buy Tax Lien Certificates in these two states. One of the most important things you will need to do before you start investing in Tax Lien Certificates is hire a very adept Certified Public Accountant. Make sure that it is someone who is savvy at preparing taxes in all aspects and anything relating to finances. Always choose a CPA who is hired for a fee not a commission. It's essential they are savvy in Tax Lien Certificates. Trying to find a CPA adept in Tax Lien Certificates might be difficult, so you might have to educate your CPA on Tax Lien Certificates and make sure he fills in the other areas, meaning he takes care of all the other tax planning and financial planning.

Once you start investing in Tax Liens Certificates, you will make a lot of money, but the number one rule is make sure you pay your taxes or you will encounter big problems with the Internal Revenue Service:(IRS) YOU DON'T WANT THAT!!!. I am giving you the basic information about Tax Lien Certificates so that you can utilize and prosper from them in the future.

Chapter 3
This Is Great – I Need to Know More

Everything that has happened had to happen. Everything that must happen cannot be stopped. –Dwayne Dyer

A lot of people might be reluctant to invest in Tax Lien Certificates because they are basically capitalizing off an individual's adversity. If you look at it like that, there wouldn't be anyone working for an income in the world everyone would be working for free. If you don't buy the Tax Lien Certificate, the government will make sure they get their money from the delinquent taxes with penalties added. No matter what, the property owner will have to pay the amount owed for the taxes on the property. Look at it like this, you are giving the property owner consignment and you are gaining interest by doing that.

Property owners will be allowed a substantial amount of time before a Tax Lien Certificate holder tries to redeem the property. Every state has a redemption period and they vary from state from state. Every state has laws that give property owners time to pay their taxes, penalties, expenses, and interest, this provides them with an opportunity to keep their property.

As a Tax Lien Certificate holder, you will never have to collect fees owed to you. The government will take care of that for you. You can relax and wait patiently for your check. The property owner pays the money directly to the county. Once the payment is made, the county will quickly send you a check for what you paid for the Tax Lien Certificate. Actually, you will get more, depending on how much the interest rate is in the state.

Technology plays a major part in business these days, which means that in most states you won't get a Tax Lien Certificate; instead, it will be logged in the computer. Then the county or state will send you a receipt displaying proof that you are the owner of that particular Tax Lien Certificate.

Once the owner of the property pays the taxes that are delinquent, the county doesn't have to delay paying you. This means even if you haven't returned your Tax Lien Certificate, they will still issue you your check. This procedure will work in your favor. It gets no easier than this.

Keep in mind, once you buy the Tax Lien Certificate it doesn't make you the owner of that specific property. To make it very simple, you are now officially acting in place of the government or county. The money the property owners pay will be the taxes and other monetary penalties that will be issued to you. Now if the property owner doesn't pay the taxes by the redemption period, you can push for foreclosure on that property.

Tax Lien Certificates are sold in twenty-eight states. Some states operate different from others. In some states you can purchase Tax Lien Certificates, while other states are deed states that sell the property itself for taxes. In some cases, the deed states can have better incentives than states that sell Tax Lien Certificates. The states that offer deeds have rules that are totally different from states that sell Tax Lien Certificates. States that sell Tax Lien Certificates offer guaranteed interest rates. Deed states don't offer that, so before you purchase property in a deed state make sure you get some legal advice from a real estate lawyer.

The procedure the county uses to determine how much taxes are owed on property is called valorem. This is when the county assesses taxes on property. The total of the taxes is based on the value of the property. Each property will vary because of the different formula used on each particular property.

The method the county begins with is the fair market value. The fair market value is the value of the property when it is actually placed on the market to be sold. By comparing other properties in the proximity that have been sold, the County Assessor comes up with the value of the property.

Let me give you an analogy. Say, for instance, that you have a house in a Beverly Hills neighborhood and it's a mini mansion. The small mansion will be compared to other houses recently sold in that neighborhood. These comparisons are called comparable, or comps in real estate language.

The county has another strategy to attain what they call a county constant. The fair market value is multiplied by this county constant to arrive at an assessed value. The county constant will be more than likely listed on a county listing of Tax Lien Certificates presented to the public for sale. The county constant is different from the initial value of the property. The majority of the time, the fair market value is ten times more than the assessed value of all the properties in the county, and the amount of revenue taken into consideration to arrive at a mill (one tenth of a cent) levy.

Once the mill levy is multiplied by the assessed value of the property, the county arrives at the dollar amount of taxes due. The calculation in this process can get complicated, so I will make it as simple as I can.

Let me give you an example. County ABC has a county constant of .09 and the mill levy is .12. Let's say a two family-flat has a fair market value of $100,000. The county will multiply the value of the county constant of .09 which will come to an assessed value of $9000 ($100,000 x .09 = $9000).

What I'm doing is getting you to see that the fair market value is more than ten times the assessed value. In most cases it might not be ten times the assessed value five times is more standard.

Keep in mind that fair market value and the assessed value are different. Now the county multiplies the assessed value by the mill levy of .12 in order to arrive at the taxes due on that property. After the equation is assessed, the amount due is going to be $1080 ($9,000 x .12 = $1080). You won't be required to know this, so you don't have to clutter your brain with these calculations. I'm just showing you how the county arrives at the amount of money owed on property taxes. This lesson can be extremely helpful to you when you are reviewing a list of Tax Lien Certificates that are for sale; potentially preventing you from being cheated out of your money.

Once the total tax amount has been finalized, a bill will be sent to the property owner revealing the amount of taxes that are due and explaining the assessed value. If the property owner feels that the bill is inaccurate or unfair, the owner can go to the Tax Assessor's Office to review the file on the property. The file will have the recent history of the property, including the width and height, the past owners, the kind of framework, etc.

You will be able to find out exactly how the county came up with the total assessment. If you still beg to differ with the total of assessment, there is an appeal process. The results typically do not favor the property owner. Usually, once a property owner receives a tax bill in which he or she is pleased with the accuracy of the assessment, they normally waste no time paying the tax bill.

In most cases some people who own homes have mortgages and the homeowner agrees to pay the mortgage company. This will allow the mortgage company to collect the monthly mortgage and place it in an escrow account.

In this agreement, the mortgage company is allowed to pay the homeowner's taxes from the escrow account, but they have to make sure their mortgage is being paid as well as the taxes. You can't trust someone else to pay your bills; therefore, it is imperative that you pay close attention to who pays your bills and where your money is going. If for some reason the mortgage company gets over on you, it will be your fault.

Please see the redemption period list below for multiple states.

Alabama - The redemption period is 3 years.

Florida - The redemption period is 2 years.

Indiana - The redemption period is 1 year, 12 days for a county purchasing agent, or county having a consolidated city.

Louisiana - The redemption period is 3 years.

Mississippi - The redemption period is 2 years.

New Hampshire- The redemption period is 2 years.

North Dakota - The redemption period is 3 years.

Arizona - The redemption period is 3 years.

Georgia - The redemption period is one year, but it's not a tax lien state.

Iowa - The redemption period is 21 months.

Maryland - The redemption period is 2 to 6 months.

Missouri - The redemption period is 2 years.

New Jersey - The redemption period is 2 years.

Oklahoma - The redemption period is 2 years.

Colorado - The redemption period is 3 years.

Illinois - The redemption period is 6 months, 2 years, to 2 ½ years.

Kentucky- None

Massachusetts- The redemption period is 6 months.

Nebraska- The redemption period is 3 years.

New York- The redemption period varies.

Rhode Island- The redemption period is 1 year.

South Carolina - The redemption period is 1 year.

West Virginia - The redemption period is 18 months.

South Dakota - The redemption period is 3 years for city property and the redemption period is 4 years for rural property.

Wyoming - The redemption period is 4 years.

Texas - The redemption period is 2 years for homestead and for agriculture, but it's just 6 months for the others. Texas is not a lien state, but is shown because of some unusual circumstances.

Chapter 4
Where do I Begin?

Where you will sit when you are old shows where you stood in youth. –Yoruba Proverb

The state you are in clearly determines how much a taxpayer pays for being late with tax payments. Interest rates vary among counties and cities within the same state. In the state of Maryland interest rates are as low as 12% and can rise to 24%. When you own property and the taxes are not paid by the scheduled time, a lien is placed on your property. Next, you incur a penalty against the property. Then the county or state offers the Tax Lien Certificates for sale at a public auction to anyone who wants to buy it in that area, county, or state.

Most of the time, thirty days before the auction the county gathers a list of all property owners that are in the area and will offer Tax Lien Certificates for each property.

The list is usually advertised in whatever county you are in. Each year the list is placed in multiple newspapers, so you must stay abreast to see which newspaper the list will be in. To make it easier, most counties charge a small fee to send you a mailing list. Depending on what county you are in, they may also mail you a list of all properties.

The lists usually come in book format, or is a replica of the list in the newspaper. While you are waiting on the county to send you the list, a number of individuals will pay their delinquent taxes. Nonetheless, if you happen to attend an auction, they will provide you with an updated list.

During the auction the Tax Lien Certificates are sold in agreement with the laws of that county. The auction is open to the public and bids are done verbally. There will be a lot of investors there. Ordinarily most are nine-to-five workers, people on a tight budget, but some are representatives from banks who have a substantial amount of money to invest.

In order to participate in the auction, you must register in your county to get on the mailing list and obtain all the data pertaining to the auction. It's best that you do your due diligence before you go to the auction. That way, you know the rules and what you are and are not allowed to do.

Please note that getting help from the county officials is very complicated. They are not enthused about helping individuals on matters regarding auctions. As a result, if you are not knowledgeable as to how this arena works, it's a gamble trying to solicit their help. You might get lucky and run across some county employees who will try to help you; however, most of them will tell you they are only able to give you the rules and requirements of the auction. For reasons such as the ones mentioned above, you may want to be one of the first to arrive on auction day. This will allow you some extra time to decide what properties you are interested in bidding on.

Make sure that you thoroughly investigate everything about the properties that have captured your interest. Put together a list of potential liens that you will be buying. Try to make your list based on prices you can afford. Also, be sure the list of properties will fit your standards.

Once you create your list, you will then have to rank the properties and eliminate the ones that do not come in as your top choices. If residential property is your area of interest, you should look at the legal description and locate properties that have the word "additions" in that legal description. If for any reason you cannot locate this information in the city, look for subdivisions. These are subdivided properties and they will include both residential and commercial properties.

In order to locate these properties, you will need a map. These maps are called plat maps and they are usually acquired at the offices of the county clerk and county appraiser, and city hall. Investors that are interested in investing in undeveloped lands should get a county grid map. It displays the township and range numbers. It also helps you find each township in your county and information on undeveloped land. The employees at the county office that gives you the map will be able to explain how to read the map. They get paid to inform you, so make sure you get them to explain it precisely.

Once you get the map, pinpoint all the properties you will be seeking. Only focus on the properties you can afford. Don't waste your time trying to seek properties you cannot afford. Once you note the properties you want, I suggest you go check each of them out to ensure that they are quality properties.

Afterwards, you'll go to the County Clerk's office and investigate if they have IRS liens or any other judgements. In some counties you can request information from the county recorder, and ask to look at the lien book to see where the IRS liens are documented. The main objective for purchasing Tax

Lien Certificates is to make a decent profit. Obtaining properties won't come easy, but it definitely can be accomplished.

The best way to earn huge profits is to purchase tax liens in wealthy areas in the suburbs. Property owners with mortgages usually pay the tax lien immediately because they don't want to lose their property; therefore, you will get paid much sooner.

No matter what, you should always try to obtain properties through tax sales and purchase Tax Lien Certificates on empty lands. The reason I suggest this is because there is always a chance you will take possession of that property. One of the most prominent matters you need to scrutinize is whether the property owners have a federal or state income tax lien documented for not paying their taxes.

These two liens are superlative to a property tax lien. The County Clerk can assist you with finding out if the properties you seek have income tax liens filed.

A lot of vacant land can come with problems such as environmental issues that can be very costly. So you have to fully look into this matter. Hiring an environmental attorney for this matter can be a headache and pricey. The best bet is to avoid properties that have these issues.

Here is a way you can have a higher chance of being successful when it comes to purchasing Tax Lien Certificates. Basically, you will have a greater chance obtaining the property in the future. To try to achieve this goal, you must purchase certificates on properties in resort or vacation subdivisions.

On some occasions people purchase these properties with the intention of one day owning a vacation home or retirement home on the property. Unfortunately, in life things don't always go as planned. To get information about these subdivisions, all you have to do is contact the realtor, broker, or someone in the sales office who's familiar with the real estate market in the proximity.

When you are in pursuit of buying Tax Lien Certificates, you need to find out how to go about purchasing it and the exact time to do so. You need to find out all this information before you start anything. Make sure you find out exactly how they distribute the certificates once you purchase them. The distribution method varies from county to county. Some send them through the mail, while other counties keep them stored in the computer where they give a receipt showing proof of ownership.

In each state, the auction dates vary, so the best thing to do is exercise due diligence in whatever state or county you are in. If you just so happen to miss the dates of the auction, there is no need to worry because once the auction is done, there will be certificates unpurchased in most counties. You can go buy them in tax offices, treasurer's offices, or by mail. Buying through the mail has proven to be the best procedure because you don't have to bid or pay auction fees. Actually, it is wise to contact your county and ask for a list of all their rules and policies.

Once you purchase a tax lien, the state creates a redemption period. Property owners are entitled to pay the taxes before the due date. At the end of this period, if you're the owner of the certificate, this is when one can exercise his right to foreclose and obtain property.

During the redemption period, most property owners pay their taxes expeditiously. The owner not only pays the taxes but also pays penalties, interest, and other expenses the county imposes. In most cases certificates are taken care of within a week or so. Some property owners wait until the last day of the redemption period. The best formula to follow in Tax Lien Certificates is once the property owner pays the taxes and other fees, you should invest your money back in for a bigger profit. The main goal is to keep accumulating wealth from this investment.

Once the county receives the payment from the property owner, they will contact you and inform you of the payment and you will have to give up the certificate. After that they will issue you a check. The counties that have the certificates placed in your computer data will automatically send you a check because they are in possession of the certificate. The redemption period varies state by state, (see chart, Chapter 3) so you have to inquire about the states you are interested in. Some are longer than others.

Again, if the property owner does not pay by the redemption period, you now have the right to foreclose. It's best to get a real estate lawyer or get the county you are in to foreclose for you. The fee varies, so you will have to contact the county you're in about the cost.

Now if by any chance the county can't do it for you, you will have to hire a lawyer who specializes in Tax Liens or a real estate lawyer, which will be more expensive but well worth it. The good part about it, you don't have to be present. It's in your best interest that the lawyer specializes in tax liens or that he is a real estate lawyer. If the lawyer specializes in any other profession, his or her services are not needed.

Don't let having to pay real estate lawyers be an issue. In the long run it will be well worth it. Let's say you have taxes on a residential property with a fair market value of $100,000. That means, according to the example I used previously, the taxes on that property would be ($9,000 x .12=$1,080). Now let's say you bought the tax lien certificate for $1,080 and the real estate lawyer cost you $4500. Altogether, the total for the lawyer and the amount paid for the Tax Lien Certificate is $5,580. Once the foreclosure is final you will have a piece of property worth $100,000 and all you paid was $5,580. That is a tremendous way to make a huge profit.

Some states are even better. You won't even have to go through the procedure of foreclosing. Colorado is a state where you don't have to go through the foreclosure procedure. Once you obtain a piece of property, all you would have to do is apply for a treasurer's deed through the county treasurer's office, because the property owner did not pay the taxes by the redemption period. You can either rent the house out or sell it, the choice is yours.

Chapter 5

WHAT YOU SHOULD KNOW
ABOUT AUCTIONS

Before you run, check to see if the bulldog has teeth. –Les Brown

It is always wise to get in contact with the County Treasure or County Clerk for the proper procedures of an auction. Usually when looking at the information for an auction, the date, time, and location will be disclosed. After that there will be a part that tells you how the county receives its income.

Every county's rules vary pertaining to a deposit some want a deposit before the sale so you have to do your research. Usually, there will be two-locations one to make deposits on the opening day of the auction and the other location if a deposit was made before the opening auction day.

Most counties will take personal checks but they must be validated with approval from your bank. At public auctions no seats will be reserved, so it's best to be punctual. I recommend arriving an hour before opening time. The public auctions are fair to all customers. A buyer data form is required and must be completed precisely.

After the form is completed and your deposit is confirmed, you will be issued a bidder number and a card. The majority of the counties have similar cards and during the open bidding, all you have to do is raise your card to have your bid acknowledged.

Once you enter the auction you will receive a fresh new list, an updated version of the list that was posted in the newspaper. I say that because the list will be put in the newspaper 30 days before the auction.

Let me give you an example. I have a list of 15 properties. Say you total up the fifteen properties from pages 39 & 40 at an assessed value, and each property is worth $40,000 so $40,000x15=$600,000 and that's a conservative estimate. Now let's say you buy all the Tax Lien Certificates for only $47,000. If that is the case, that means you would have $503,000 worth of real estate and you only paid $47,000.

You can't beat that. Wise up people. The assessed value is $600,000. Keep in mind that the fair market value is at least ten times larger. Keep in mind this is a very safe investment.

The interest rate in New Jersey is 18%. Usually at auctions in New Jersey, or any other state, people will try to outbid you, but that's not the case all the time. Sometimes you might be the only person bidding. In most cases the Tax Lien Certificates will outweigh the investors. The example I used earlier about the fifteen properties is from a real tax lien list. Actually, it was left over Tax Lien Certificates from an auction in Ewing, NJ. I gained access from the tax office in Ewing Township.

The benefits you get from the left over certificates are very rewarding. You don't have to worry about people bidding against you and you don't have to worry about paying any extra fees. Before going to an auction, always have a list of the properties you want to bid on, then set a limit you won't exceed when you are bidding. This will keep you from paying more for a property than you planned to.

Please See the Table Below...

Ewing Township Tax Lien List

14	581	*1	3	Leneus,Edrick	8 New Trent St	3,208.68	Township Of Ewing	18
14	582	2	1	Carter, Shirley A.	207 New Trent St	215.84	Township Of Ewing	18
14	583	2	3	Jones, Stephen & Bessie	194 W Ingham Ave	2,774.13	Township Of Ewing	18
14	584	*3	16	TLR-V, LLC/18th Floor	526 W Ingham Ave	3,692.42	Township Of Ewing	18
14	585	13	31	Mikkelsen, Michael C.	1555 N Olden Ave Ext	2,905.79	Township Of Ewing	18
14	586	*17	14	Sulikowski, Maria	46 Stout Ave	3,334.46	Township Of Ewing	18
14	587	*21	9(10)	De Lorenzo Salvatore UX	242 Stokes Ave	7,169.89	Township Of Ewing	18
14	588	*21. 01	53	Smith And Pineda, LLC	429 Hazel Ave	2,686.97	Township Of Ewing	18

14	589	*23	2	Sciangola, Lawrence J.	1000 Prospect St	1,187.95	Township Of Ewing	18
14	590	30	304.02	Hoagland, Jr. William R.	233 Robbins Ave	653.02	Township Of Ewing	18
14	591	30	304.03	Hoagland Jr. William R.	235 Robbins Ave	653.02	Township Of Ewing	18
14	592	34	498 (499-501)	Lazo, Jose	58 Weber Ave	4,203.09	Township Of Ewing	18
14	593	42	6(11)	Local Union AFL-CIO Local 17	42 Artic Parkway	4,697.79	Township Of Ewing	18
14	594	51	220.02	Depaola R&D (DBA) Schoolhouse	1751 Sixth St	1,506.86	Township Of Ewing	18
14	595	*118 .02	106	Chang & Jung Inc. A NJ. Cor	1812 N Olden Ave Ext	9,077.6	Township Of Ewing	18

Total Amount to Township   **$47,967.57**

Once you purchase a Tax Lien Certificate, you become the certificate holder. If the property owner doesn't redeem the property taxes they will continue to accrue and you will now be responsible for paying them. The property owner has to pay you all of the taxes and any other fees you included.

The good thing about paying the annual taxes is that you get closer to owning the property. Now, if you don't pay the annual taxes, the county will convey the certificate to someone else. If the new owner of the Tax Lien Certificate forecloses due to neglect of the property, the lien will be eliminated.

All the people that have an interest in any property will be informed by the Treasurer and after two years or maybe sooner than that in New Jersey, you will become the owner of the property. Even if the owner recovers the property, the county will pay you 18% in interest on your investment.

When it comes to auctions, most of them do not divulge that much information, so you have to ask questions on your own. Case in point, in Colorado premium bidding is used and the premium is held by the county.

Once the property owner pays the taxes, they are not entitled to pay the premium, so the premium decreases your profit. Say for example you pay a premium in order to buy a Tax Lien Certificate and the property owner pays the taxes in a few days. Since Colorado has a premium bidding system, the buyers bid on the additional fees they are willing to pay for the Tax Lien Certificate. This exceeds the original amount due, regarding the taxes recorded on the list.

In this example the interest rate will be paid, but no interest will be paid on the premium. In Colorado, they use what you call the rotational bidding process. For example, card 1 goes first, then card 2, and it continues in that order around the room. Being as though the auction is crowded, you won't be able to bid as you like.

You can use a stratagem by bringing your significant other, a family member, your sister etc. Then you can also register a company you own and it will be assigned a number. The people in your company will now often have a turn to bid. Keep in mind that each company or person will have to make a deposit in his or her name. Then at the end you can convey and sell all the certificates you buy to whatever company is beneficial to you.

Chapter 6

Different Strategies at the Auction

There are three kinds of people in the world, those who make
things happen, those who watch things happen, those who
wonder what happened. – Unknown

There are more ways than one to bid for Tax Lien
Certificates; in Colorado, bidders bid up to the amount they are
willing to pay. In many other states, bidders bid down the actual
interest rate.

The state of Florida has an interest rate of 18%. The
person who bids for the lowest interest rate is successful in
acquiring the Tax Lien Certificate. The bid will start at 18%, and
bidders will continuously offer lower interest rates as a bid, from
18% to 17.35%, as an example. The bidding will continue until
the person willing to accept the lowest interest rate becomes the
successful bidder, and therefore the owner of the certificate.

Many auctions are held in various counties. At times,
some counties will have over 5,000 Tax Lien Certificates up for
auction at one time. Many times, because of the excess of
certificates and the small number of bidders present, the majority
of the certificates go for the opening interest bid. Regardless of
what a bidder gets as their interest rate in a Tax Lien Certificate,

any difference between the state's interest rate and their bid goes directly to the county.

Nevertheless, the bidder get an investment that's completely secured for a very lucrative return. Even if a bidder were to settle for a low interest rate (say 15%) that person would still have a totally secure investment that will double in less than five years.

Remember that as an investor, you have all of the information pertaining to rates of return from the beginning and those rates are flexible. You are in control, so select the rate that works best for you.

Tax Lien Certificates are the only safe form of investment that is completely secured by real estate. The stock market and even mutual funds are not secured investments. If an investor puts $4,000 a year in any mutual fund investment for at least twenty years, more than likely, by the end of the twenty years, the account would depreciate due to the unstableness of the stock market.

If the same investor invested at Florida's 18% rate, after twenty years the account would check in at a little under $300,000. Other states have even higher interest rates, such as Iowa (24%) and Texas (25%). An investor's options are very flexible.

Iowa's annual rate is 24%, they pay 2% every month, making it one of the best states to buy Tax Lien Certificates. An investor in Iowa, after a certificate is redeemed, receives their full investment plus 2% per month.

Investors bid on the undivided interest of the property. Whoever is willing to take the lowest percentage wins the bid. Upon foreclosure, an investor would own only the percentage of the property they bid for. Usually, this means nothing because foreclosure is so rare. In the event of a foreclosure, the investor usually makes even more money because of their partial ownership of the property that has been foreclosed on. Either way, the investor is capitalizing on their investment.

Chapter 7
Have You Learned A Lot Yet?

If you always do what you always did, you will always get what you always got. – Jackie "Moms" Mabley

You have to treat this book as a study guide; you must read it over and over. All of the information in this book will help you gain profit on your tax lien investments. The majority of the revenue from a county comes from taxes that are assessed relating to real estate, which is known as an ad valorem tax. It is called that because it's assessed on the value of the property.

There are all kinds of property involved, including commercial property, industrial property, raw land, single and multifamily residential property. To determine the value regarding real estate, the County Tax Assessor will estimate the value to real estate, and then multiply the value by a predetermined county constant to arrive at an assessed value. The assessor then multiplies this assessed value by a county constant and the result of this method becomes the amount of taxes the owner of the property must pay.

If the owner of the property doesn't pay on time it creates a financial deficit in the operating revenue needed to satisfy the operations of the county.

It is the county's right to collect the taxes or seize the property. Unfortunately, it won't happen right away. A redemption period is set by the state legislature, so property owners can bring their taxes up to date without losing their property, which happens in 98% of these kind of cases.

In every state the redemption period varies. In most states the redemption period starts at six months and goes up to five years. Five years is too long for the counties to receive their operating revenue. Most counties in the U.S depend on private investors to provide the funds. This is done by creating a Tax Lien Certificate.

The certificate offers proof that the property owner is delinquent with their taxes. It also gives the owner of this certificate all the same rights the county has. The state legislature establishes a penalty that must be collected by the county against delinquent taxpayers. This penalty is in the form of a rate of interest that must be paid on the amount of delinquent taxes. The penalties range from 8% to as much as 50%.

The certificates are sold by the county to private investors at public auctions. Some counties carry out auctions once a year. Other counties may hold several auctions during the course of the year. These are public auctions that anyone can attend and any one can bid except for employees of the county conducting the auction.

The certificates start as low as $50. Many of the auctions are ran the same as any auction you may have attended, such as a car auction, or a fine art auction. Some counties differ from the norm, but the following is the usual auction routine.

You register for the auction prior to the start date and you are assigned a bidding number. This number is printed on a card and you simply hold up the card when you bid. As I stated before, at the auction there are several methods of bidding. In some states you bid down the interest rate.

Arizona is a state that bids down. It's interest rate is 18%. So the bidder that is willing to accept the smallest interest rate will win the bid. Other states such as Colorado have premium bidding. The certificate is sold to the buyer who pays the largest amount of taxes, penalty interest, and any other fees by that particular county.

Another method, called competitive bidding, is strictly for any investor who agrees to the undivided interest in the property if foreclosure is caused. The interest rate is not lessened unless the certificate is paid off. Keep in mind they are paid off the majority of the time, and you, the investor will get the profit from the interest rate. Here is a description of how each state operates in the bidding process at auctions:

Alabama
In Alabama, you bid up at the auction. The investor will bid on the total of the certificate and the investor who has the highest amount over the original amount due will win the bid. In Alabama, any remaining money will go back to the investor (bidder) when the property owner redeems the house. If the owner doesn't redeem the property, the county keeps the extra money.

Arizona

Arizona is a state where you bid down the interest rate. The investor who agrees to the lowest rate wins.

Colorado

In Colorado you bid up, which causes you to bid over the total amount of taxes and fees owed. The person who is willing to pay the most for the premium becomes the buyer. The issue with this is that the county keeps the extra fees and the property owner pays no interest on the extra fees.

Florida

Florida is a bid down state. There you bid down to the rate until you find one that is agreeable.

Georgia

In Georgia, you bid up and once the owner redeems the property the investor gets the premium reimbursed to him or her from the county. If foreclosure takes place, the county keeps the remaining balance.

Illinois

Illinois is a bid down state.

Indiana

In Indiana, you bid up. The leftover money goes to the investor at the redemption, but the county keeps the leftover money if foreclosure takes place.

Iowa
In Iowa, you bid on an undivided interest. The person who agrees to the lowest percentage of undivided interest in the property wins the bid. That person is then officially a joint owner with the original property owner.

Kentucky
Kentucky has a rare way of bidding. The Tax Lien Certificates are sold by lottery. A lottery is held to select the buyer if there is more than one person who is interested in buying a lien.

Louisiana
In Louisiana you bid on an undivided interest.

Maryland
Maryland is a bid up state. If you want the property, the excess bid is sold on credit.

Massachusetts
Massachusetts is an undivided interest state.

Missouri

Missouri is a bid up state. The excess goes back to the investor if redeemed.

Nebraska

Nebraska is an undivided interest state.

New Hampshire

New Hampshire is an undivided interest state.

New Jersey

New Jersey is a bid down state.

New York

Each county varies. Due diligence is required as New York is a complicated state.

North Dakota

North Dakota is a bid down state.

Oklahoma

Oklahoma is another lottery state.

South Dakota

South Dakota is a bid down state.

West Virginia

West Virginia is a bid up state. The excess goes to the investor at redemption, but the surplus does not earn interest.

Wyoming

Wyoming is a lottery state. When your number is drawn, you buy or pass.

I have done my best to give you a sufficient amount of information, but there might be more information you'll need to attain. The best thing to do is to gather up all the information I have given you and contact the counties and states you are interested in pursuing Tax Lien Certificates in.

Once you become an owner of a Tax Lien Certificate you will pay for your investment according to the rules of that county. After that, the county will mail you a certificate, usually in a few days. Some states keep the certificates in their computer and a receipt will be given.

In most cases the property owner is going to go to the county tax office and pay the tax lien. The county employee will collect all the money due, which includes taxes, fees, and any other penalties.

Once they mail you the certificate, they will inform you that the taxes have been paid and ask you to turn over the certificate. Tax Lien Certificates are very valuable; therefore, they should be kept somewhere safe. If lost, you will have to pay for a new copy. Charges are from $10 and up.

If the county has the certificate in the computer, all they would have to do is mail you the check. Avoiding auctions and competitive bidding will get you the maximum return on your investment. This is called Assignment Purchases. To find the remaining Tax Lien Certificates, just call the county in the state you want to invest in to see if they have any leftover certificates. When you buy the leftover certificates, most of them are closer to the redemption date.

If the property owner doesn't pay the taxes during the redemption period, you proceed to foreclosure. In most states you go through a foreclosure process. For this you can hire an attorney or you can get the county to do it for a small fee. In some states, like Colorado, you just make an application to the County Treasurer for a Treasurer's Deed.

Chapter 8
Things You Should Know

You must act as if it is impossible to fail. – Ashanti Proverb

There are a lot of reasons for property owners to stay current with their taxes. The main reason is that being delinquent can cost them their property.

Most property owners die without creating a will and the county ends up owning the property. There are also instances in which some who have property willed to them and may not be financially literate or informed about Tax Lien Certificates. Consequently, they might not know how important it is to pay the taxes. As a result, they end up letting the property go.

Sometimes property owners figure that because there might be some problems with the property, it is cheaper to just lose the property than to take on the financial burden. The federal government passed a law called the Superfund Act. This law makes the current property owner responsible for cleaning up contaminated property.

Even if you weren't the one who polluted the property you still will be held responsible. No matter when you acquired the property, the government will hold you responsible.

The best way to avoid this is to stay away from industrial property. Though not all industrial property is contaminated, you just don't want to gamble. You can face the same issues with commercial properties, so be careful. Note that your best option is to buy certificates on residential properties. Your investment will be safe and you won't have any worries about pollution problems. Even buying certificates on farm land is risky, so don't gamble your money on them either.

Let's say a property owner has been sued in civil court and the person or company who brought the suit has won a judgement. There may be a lien filed against the property owner on everything the person or company owns. This lien would cause a problem for anyone trying to get the title to any property that person owned. The property owner will have to pay this lien before anyone can obtain a clear title to the property. Also, the property owner can't sell the property until the lien is cleared.

The good thing is, if you are in a situation like this and you foreclose on a property with a lien, you won't have an issue. This kind of lien is junior to a tax lien and will be exterminated by foreclosure. As long as you follow the proper procedures, you will take 100% of the property. Yet, as mentioned before, to be on the safe side, hire a lawyer. It's best to check to see if the lien is taken off after the foreclosure. To be safe it's also best for you to purchase title insurance, and then the title company will inspect for any liens that may be on the property. It's the title company's responsibility to defend that title and protect you.

In some states title companies will issue a title policy on tax-forfeited land after one year if the property owner doesn't claim the property. Some states may require a quiet title action.

Contact a title company in the area where you own property and ask them to explain how this whole ordeal is handled.

Once you become a property owner by buying a tax lien certificate you probably will want to sell the property quickly; therefore, it's best for you to get title insurance immediately since most people require title insurance. Ultimately, you will have to find a company that issues title insurance for an affordable price.

Usually, state and municipal tax liens are removed once you foreclose on any property. If by any chance you face an issue about a lien still remaining, then you have to contact a lawyer in the state where you have this issue for assistance. IRS liens and federal tax liens are senior to Tax Lien Certificates. If you obtain property, you will obtain the lien also. As long as you follow the method that the IRS wants you to follow, they will remove the liens. Contact the county officials or contact the IRS. It's important to talk with the highest person in command to ensure that you get the right answers.

Always remember, if you bid on Tax Lien Certificates or buy a Tax Lien Certificate, be sure to check for IRS liens and federal tax liens. Keep in mind that some people will pay their tax liens and recover their property. For this reason, you want to buy a lot of tax liens just in case others are paid off. This will give you a chance to obtain the property. But still, no matter what, your money will always be working for you.

When buying Tax Lien Certificates, never spend money you can't afford to lose. Always have money saved for a rainy day long before you seek a profit from this investment because you will have to pay the annual taxes until the redemption period is over. If you don't pay the taxes, your Tax Lien Certificate will be sold. If you were to ever get in a jam and you can't afford to pay the annual taxes, there are companies that will sell your Tax Lien Certificates for you.

You can contact your local tax office for these companies. In cases where a county makes a mistake by letting you buy a tax lien that has a bankruptcy on it, the county will issue your money back to you and some will also pay you interest since they made the error.

If you buy a Tax Lien Certificate and the property owner declares bankruptcy, even though the bankruptcy procedures will wipe out the individual's debt, it won't remove your Tax Lien Certificate. Your investment is secured. The worst thing that could happen is that it might take longer to sell the property, especially if you have to foreclose. With the profit you gain from this investment, it's worth the wait. If you are ever in a situation where the property owner declares bankruptcy, you must carefully read everything you received from Bankruptcy Court.

At that point, you must file a claim on what is called a Proof of Claim of Bankruptcy Form. Just in case the courts don't send one, call them to find out where you can pick one up. If you obtain a piece of property because the owner didn't redeem it, you must hire a real estate lawyer to handle the foreclosure because you will be responsible for receiving all notices from that particular county.

An improper notice can void the foreclosure and cause you to lose the property. Even if you run into a piece of property that no one wants, don't panic. You can donate that property to charity, and use it as a tax write off. All you have to do is find out the Fair Market Value of the property. That information can be obtained from the tax office. Make sure you decide what states and countries you want to buy Tax Lien Certificates in before you invest. Make sure you are precise.

Say for example, you live in New Jersey and the interest rate is 18% and the redemption period is two years. As a result of this, you might not want to invest in that state. Based on your research, you find out that Maryland's interest rate is 18%, but the redemption period is six months. If you make a decision to invest in Maryland, you have a better chance of obtaining someone's property if they don't pay the tax lien by the redemption period. This is a good example of why it's good to research all states.

Chapter 9
Executing the Steps to Making a lot of Money

I cannot win anything, until I am willing to lose everything. –
Kennedy Schultz

Most of the people who buy this book primarily want to invest in Tax Lien Certificates. Most will have their own strategy, but some won't. Some people will invest through a self-directed IRA or some other retirement plan. Others just might make this a business. The most important thing you must do is take advantage of the information in this book and buy Tax Lien Certificates.

If you don't, you will be doing yourself a big disservice. All the information in this book is accurate, so there is no excuse for you not to take advantage of this opportunity. If you make Tax Lien Certificates a business, whenever you have to travel for business-related issues, it is tax deductible.

The deductions only apply if you have an official business, in which all of your travel is truly pertaining to Tax Lien Certificates. For more information, contact an accountant.

As long as you meet the requirements for a home business, you can deduct a portion of your house payments, insurance, taxes, phone bill, utilities, etc. If you do start a home-based business, you have to have your records in order before you file your tax returns, and make sure it is done in a timely manner.

Also, if traveling in your vehicle, please note that the mileage can be tax deductible as long as it is business related. The government pays .51 cents per mile. You must keep a ledger of your mileage for IRS audits. If done properly, you can get a tax write-off for several things that most people are unaware are available to them. Just ask your accountant how. If you buy a computer for your business or house, you can deduct the entire cost the first year as a business expense.

It's essential that you have an experienced accountant take care of these matters. You should never hire an accountant who won't fight to get you the deductions that you are entitled to. When investing in Tax Lien Certificates, it's wise to build a rapport with your banker so that you can take advantage of using financial leverage. This means you will have an opportunity to borrow from your bank and make an investment in Tax Lien Certificates.

Basically, this will put you in a position to negotiate with your bank an interest rate you and your lender both agree to. For example, let's say you pay your banker 9% and you buy Tax Lien Certificates in Maryland for 18%. You may not realize this, but you would earn an extra 9% interest by using the bank's money. You can do the same with your credit card.

Some auctions allow investors to use their credit cards in order to get a cash advance. If investors buy tax liens on property with short redemption periods that have an interest rate greater than what their card company is charging, it can be another benefit.

Keep in mind, it is important not to make these kind of investments unless you can afford the monthly payments. Make sure you weigh your options. If you feel like you can make a decent profit by borrowing money from the bank, then proceed with the transaction; however, be sure to clearly think out the pros and cons before you make a decision.

A good way to start saving money and to invest in Tax Lien Certificates is to save $250 a month for one year and by the twelfth month, you will have reached $3000. Once you get the $3000, you could invest it in Tax Lien Certificates. Another thing you can do is save your income tax refund check. Finally, you can also save for a few additional months until you reach $3000.

If you are in New Jersey or Maryland and you invested $3000 in Tax Lien Certificates, within 20 years you should have well over $200,000. Keep in mind, you have to continue investing in Tax Lien Certificates and you can't spend the profit. Keep investing the profit and your money will increase. Remember, don't use your last $3000 to invest. When buying Tax Liens, it should be with money you won't realize is gone.

If you invest and start spending the profit, then you are defeating the purpose, and you won't see any significant results.

The information in this book is very powerful. It is full of resourceful material that you can use to elevate your future financial status. Even if you can't save $3000, you can start with $2000, $1500, $1000, $500, $300, even $100. It doesn't cost that much to attend an auction. It will also be cheaper for you to find a county that has leftover Tax Lien Certificates. Please don't procrastinate on getting this done. Go to the nearest County Courthouse or City Hall in your state and get a Tax Lien list to see what Tax Lien Certificates are available.

Also, while you are there, get familiar with the record books and start your research. Ask the people that work in these offices all of the questions you need to ask to ensure that you become more educated on Tax Lien Certificates.

Chapter 10
I Know I Will Get a Good Return off My Money but I Want the Property

If you want to be a millionaire, you have to think like one –
Dr. Johnnie Coleman

If you want to increase the chances of obtaining property and increasing the yield on your investment, you have to go to a state that assesses the penalty in full. Texas is a state that does that. Texas is not a Tax Lien Certificate State. Texas has what is called a Tax Deed Certificate. Once you buy the Tax Deed Certificate you are buying the property for the taxes due but the owner has one last chance to redeem the property before you can make it yours.

Texas assesses a penalty of 25% that is in full force and effect instantly. If the owner redeems the property the day after you buy the certificate, you still earn 25% on the full amount of the certificate even though you have only owned it for one day.

With this high interest rate, you will make a massive profit. In Texas, before you can start foreclosure procedures, the property owner has six months to redeem the property. The six-month period means that the lowest return you will receive is 50%.

No matter what, your investment is safe. Once you purchase a Tax Lien Certificate the best thing to do is write a letter to the property owner. Tell the owner that you have purchased a Tax Deed Certificate and his property is at stake. Try to inspire the owner to pay the taxes as soon as possible to avoid losing the property. If you can get them to pay instantly, you will get a giant profit on your investment. Being that it's only a six-month redemption period, your chances of obtaining the property are higher. If you don't obtain the property you still will make a huge profit from the interest rate.

If you obtain the property, you are entitled to collect rent from the property owner, if they are using or occupying the property. You can come up with a lot of strategies to improve your chances of obtaining property. One way is to try to buy a lot of Tax Lien Certificates on vacant land. For example, if you buy fifteen Tax Lien Certificates for $100, out of that fifteen, you might get lucky and get three or more vacant lands. If so, you can sell the vacant land on eBay, Angie's list, Facebook, or any other social media sites, etc.

In Georgia, they have a one-year redemption period. The interest rate is 20% and is due in full on the first day of the year. If the owner redeems on the first day of the second year, the investor has earned 40% in one year and one day.

If the investor has to have a notice of foreclosure served by the Sheriff, this adds another 20%; therefore, an investor can earn 60% in just a very short period of time. In most cases, you will end up obtaining the property in Texas and Georgia with a chance to earn 50% or even 60% in interest. You can't beat that.

As you can see, investing in Tax Lien Certificates is not as complicated as a lot of people try to make it seem. It is similar to investing in a saving account but with a much bigger interest rate.

At the end of this last chapter, I have a list of some counties in the United States where you can buy Tax Lien Certificates by going to auctions or buying them over the counter.

Some cities like Baltimore sell Tax Lien Certificates, but most Tax Lien Certificates are sold by counties. Among the listings below, I will provide you with a list of the states, and then give you the information about that state pertaining to rates, redemption periods, etc. The list will also include county listings.

I just want to remind readers that all of the information I obtained about county offices is liable to change, such as addresses and phone numbers. So, if by any chance a phone number and address has been changed, don't panic. All you have to do is call 411 for the most recent phone number and address or you can search the internet.

Don't let minor issue discourage you, if something happens to occur. There is plenty of money to be made from buying Tax Lien Certificates. Please take advantage of it. Most numbers on the listings are tax offices, but some are to the Treasurer's Office.

I would like to thank you for allowing me to enrich your mind with this vital information. Now the only thing I ask of you is to please use this information quickly so that you can start the process of success or continue to add on to your success. Unfortunately, all good things must come to an end but the beginning of your success starts once you make your first investment in Tax Lien Certificates. I wish you well in your Tax Lien Investment and anything else you set your mind to pursue in the future!

Alabama

Alabama has a statutory penalty interest rate of 12%. There is a three-year redemption period. At the end of three years, you can request and receive a Tax Deed at the auction you bid up the sale price.

Baldwin PO Box 1549 Bay Minette, AL 205-937-0245	Butler PO Box 756 Greenville, AL 205-382-3221
Calhoun 1702 Nobel St. Anninston, AL 205-237-1111	Cherokee Cherokee County Courthouse Ceutre, AL 205-927-5527
Choctaw 117 South Mulberry Street Butler, AL 205-459-2411	Clark PO Box 9 Grove Hill, AL 205-275-3377
Clay PO Box 155 Ashland, AL 205-275-3377	Cleburne 406 Vickery St. Heflin, AL 205-463-2873
Coffee 100 S. Edwards St. Enterprise, AL 205-347-8734	Colbert PO Box 1236 Tuseuwbia, AL 205-386-8538

Coosa PO Box 7 Rockford, AL 205-377-4916	Crenshaw PO Box 208 Luverne, AL 205-335-6568
Cullman PO Box 220 Cullman, AL 205-739-3535	Dale Dale County Courthouse Ozark, AL 205-774-2226
Dallas 105 Lauderdale St. Selvia, AL 205-874-2519	Elmore PO Box 396 Wetumpka, AL 205-567-1118
Franklin PO Box 248 Russellville, AL 205-332-8841	Geneva PO Box 326 Geneva, AL 205-684-3119
Greene PO Box 45 Eutaw, AL 205-372-3144	Jackson PO Box 307 Scottsboro, AL 205-574-9390
Jefferson Jefferson County Courthouse Birmingham, AL 205-325- 5500	Lauderdale PO Box 794 Florence, AL 205-760-5785
Limestone Limestone County Courthouse Athens, AL 205-233-6435	Macon 101 E. Northside Tuskegee, AL 205-724-2603

Marengo	Mobile
Marengo County Courthouse	PO Box 7
Linden, AL	Mobile, AL
205-295-2214	205-690-8530
Pickens	Pike
PO Box 447	Pike County Courthouse
Carrollton, AL	Troy, AL
205-367-2040	205-566-1792
Russell	St. Clair
PO Box 669	PO Box 1129
Phenix City, AL	Ashville, AL
205-298-6661	204-594-5143
Sumter	Tuscaloosa
PO Box DD	Tuscaloosa County Courthouse
Livingston, AL	Greensboro, AL
205-652-2251	205-359-3870

Arizona

Arizona has a statutory penalty interest rate of 16%. Sale dates are in February and vary by county. Bid down the interest rate. Certificates will go to a person willing to accept the lowest interest rate. You can purchase by mail with no bidding down after the tax sale. Foreclosure is a little easier after 5 years.

Apache	Cochise
PO Box 669	PO Box 1778
St. Johns, AZ 89536	Bisbee, AZ 85603
520-337-4364	520-432-9322

Coconino 100 East Birch St Flagstaff, AZ 86001 520-779-6615	Graham 800 Main St Safford, AZ 85546 520-428-3440
Gila 1400 East Ash St. Globe, AZ 85501 520-425-3231	Greenlee PO Box 1227 Clifton, AZ 85533 520-865-3422
Lapaz PO Box BQ Parker, AZ 85344 520-669-6145	Maricopa 301 West Jefferson Phoenix, AZ 85003 620-506-8511
Mohave PO Box 712 Kingman, AZ 86401 520-753-0737	Navajo PO Box 668 Holbrook, AZ 86025 520-524-4172
Pima 110 West Congress Tucson, AZ 85701 520-740-8344	Pinal PO Box 729 Florence, AZ 85232 520-868-6425
Santa Cruz Nogales, AZ 85628 520-761-7800	Yavapai 255 East Gurley Prescott, AZ 86301 520-771-3233
Yuma Yuma, AZ 85364 520-329-2048	

Colorado

Colorado has a statutory penalty interest rate of 9% plus the Federal Discount Rate on September 1st of the year of the sale, the rate then remains consistent throughout the year for new sales. Tax Lien Certificates will continue to accrue interest at the rate set at the time of purchase. New purchase will carry the new interest rate. Keep in mind sale dates vary by county. The redemption period is 3 years.

Adams 450 S. 4th Brighton, CO 80601 303-654-6165	Arapahoe 5334 Prince St. Littleton, CO 80166 303-795-4950
Archuleta PO Box 148 Pagosa Springs, CO 81147 303-264-2152	Baca 719 741 Main St. Springfield, CO 81073
Boulder 17776th St. Boulder, CO 80306 303-441-3520	Chaffee 132 Crestone Salida, CO 81201 719-539-6808
Cheyenne 51 South First St. Cheyenne Wells, CO 80810 719-767-5657	Clear Creek PO Box 2000 Georgetown, CO 80444 303-569-3251
Conejos PO Box 127 Conejos, CO 81129 719-376-5919	Castilla PO Box 100 San Luis, CO 81151 719-672-3342
Crowley 6th and Main St. Ordway, CO 81063 719-267-4624	Custer 205 South 6th St. Westcliffe, CO 81252 719-783-2341
DeHa 501 Palmer DeHa, CO 81416 303-874-2135	Delores PO Box 614 Dove Creek, CO 81324 303-677-2386
Douglas 301 South Wilcox St. Castle Rock, CO 80104 303-660-7455	Eagle PO Box 597 Eagle, CO 81631 303-328-8860

Elbert 751 Ute St. Kiowa, CO 80117 303-621-3120	El Paso 20 East Vermijo St. Colorado Springs, CO 80903 719-520-6666
Garfield 109 8th St. Glenwood Springs, CO 81601 303-945-6382	Gilpin 203 Eureka St. Central City, CO 80247 303-582-5222
Grand PO Box 192 Hot Sulphur Springs, CO 80451 303-725-3347	Gunnison 200 E. Virginia Ave. Gunnison, CO 81230 303-641-2231
Huerfano 400 Main St. Walsenburg, CO 81089 719-738-1280	Jackson PO Box 337 Walden, CO 81089 303-723-4220
Jefferson 1701 Arapahoe St. Golden, CO 80419 303-271-8330	Kiowa PO Box 353 Eads, CO 81036 719-438-5831
Kit Carson Burlington, CO 80807 719-346-8434	Lake PO Box 55 Leadville, CO 80461 719-486-0530
LA Plata PO Box 99 Durango, CO 81302 970-382-6239	Larimer PO Box 1250 Fort Collins, CO 80522 970-498-7020
Las Animas Trinidad, CO 81082 719-846-2981	Lincoln PO Box 67 Hugo, CO 80821 719-743-2633
Logan 300 Main St. Sterling, CO 80751 303-522-2462	Mesa PO Box 200 Grand Junction, CO 81502 303-244-9183

Mineral PO Box 70 Creede, CO 81130 719-658-2575	Moffat 227 West Victory Lane Craig, Co 81625 970-824-6670
Morgan PO Box 1289 Montrose, CO 81402 303-867-5615	Otero 13 West Third St. Lajunta, CO 81050 719-384-5473
Ouray PO Box C Ouray, CO 81427 970-325-4405	Park PO Box 220 Fairplay, CO 80440 719-836-2771
Pitkin 506 Main St. Aspen, CO 81611 303-925-7635	Phillips 221 S. Interocean Ave. Holyoke, CO 80734 303-854-2822
Prowers 301 South Main Lamar, CO 81052 719-336-2081	Pueblo 211 West 10th Pueblo, CO 81003 719-583-6000
Rio Blanco PO Box G Meeker, CO 81641 970-878-3614	Routt 522 Lincoln Ave. Steamboat Springs, CO 80477 303-877-1732
Saguache PO Box 356 Saguache, CO 81149 719-655-7522	San Juan PO Box 466 Silverton, CO 81433 970-387-5488
San Miguel PO Box 919 Telluride, CO 81435 303-728-3891	Sedgwick PO Box 3 Julesburg, CO 80737 303-474-3627
Summit PO Box 868 Breckenridge, CO 80424 303-453-2561	Teller PO Box 959 Cripple Creek, CO 80720 719-689-2574

Washington	Weld
150 Ash St.	915 10th Ave.
Akron, CO 80720	Greeley, CO 80631
303-345-2756	303-356-4000
Yuma	
310 Ash	
Wray, CO 80758	
303-332-5809	

Florida

Florida has a statutory penalty interest rate of 18%. Sales dates can vary by county and from year to year. At the auction, the interest rate is bid down in ¼% increments. The successful bidder is the one accepting the lowest interest rate.

A $1,000 deposit is required and purchases are charged against this amount. Any money left over is returned within 30 days. If you purchase more than the deposit, you can pay 10% down and the balance according to county requirements. The redemption period is 2 years. After 2 years an unpaid certificate holder can apply for a Tax Deed.

Alachua	Baker
201 East University	55 North Third St.
Gainesville, FL 32602	Macclenny, FL 32063
904-374-5236	904-259-6880
Bay	Bradford
300 E. Fourth St.	945 N. Temple Ave.
Panama City, FL 32402	Starke, FL 32091
850-235-2285	904-964-6044
Brevard	Broward
700 S. Park Ave.	115 S. Andrews Ave.
Titusville, FL 32781	Fort Lauderdale, FL 33301
407-264-5283	305-468-3433

Calhoun 425 E. Central Ave. Blounstown, FL 32424 850-674-4545	Charlotte 116 W. Olympia Punta Gorda, FL 33950 813-743-1354
Citrus Inverness Hwy 41 Inverness, FL 32650 904-637-9485	Clay 825 N. Orange Ave. Green Cove Springs, FL 32043 904-269-6302
Collier 3301 Tamiami Trail Naples, FL 33962 813-774-8171	Columbia 145 N. Hernando St. Lake City, FL 32056 904-758-1080
Dade 111 NW First St. Miami, FL 33128 305-375-1790	Desoto 201 E. Oak St. Arcadia, FL 33821 813-993-4861
Dixie 351 King St. Cross City, FL 32628 904-498-1213	Duval 330 E. Bay St. Jacksonville, FL 32202 904-630-2059
Escambia 223 S. Pala Fox Place Pensacola, FL 32501 904-436-5714	Flager 200 East Moody Bunnell, FL 32010 904-437-7408
Franklin PO Box 340 Apalachicola, FL 32320 904-653-8861	Gadsden 10 E. Jefferson Quincy, FL 32351 904-627-7255
Gilchrist 904-463-3170 112 S. Main St. Trenton, FL 32693	Glades 813-946-0626 500 Ave J Moore Haven, FL 33471
Gulf 100 5th St. Port Saint Joe, FL 32456 850-639-5068	Hamilton 207 N.E 1st St. Jasper., FL 32052 904-792-1284

Hardee	Hendry
417 E. Main St.	PO Box 1760
Wauchula, FL 33873	Labelle, Florida 33935
813-773-4174	813-675-5205
Hernanco	Highlands
20 N. Main St.	430 S. Commerce
Brooksville, FL 34601	Sebring, FL 33781
904-754-4180	941-386-6565
Hillsborough	Holmes
419 Pierce St.	201 N. Oklahoma St.
Tampa, FL 33601	Bonifay, FL 32425
813-272-6000	904-547-1116
Indian River	Jackson
2864 Madison St.	4445 Lafayette St.
Vero Beach, FL 32960	Marianna, FL 32446
407-567-8000	904-482-9653
Jefferson	Lafayette
1240 N. Jefferson St.	County Court House
Monticello, FL 32344	Mayo, FL 32066
904-342-0148	904-294-1961
Lake	Lee
315 West Main St.	2115 2nd St.
Tavares, FL 32773	Fort Myers, FL 33901
904-343-9622	813-335-2317
Leon	Levy
904-488-4381	904-486-5174
301 South Moore	355 South Court St.
Tallahassee, FL 32302	Bronson, FL 32621
Liberty	Madison
P.O Box 400	112 E. Pickney
Bristol, FL 32321	Madison, FL 32340
904-643-2442	904-973-6136
Manatee	Marion
1115 Manatee Ave. W	110 NW 1st Ave.
Bradenton, FL 33506	Cala, FL 34475
813-741-4820	904-288-5746

Martin 100 East Ocean Blvd. Stuart, FL 33494 407-288-5746	Monroe 500 Whitehead St. Key West, FL 33040 305-294-8403
Nassau 416 Center St. Fernandina Beach, FL 32034 904-261-5566	Okaloosa 101 E. James Lee Blvd Crestview, FL 32536 904-689-5700
Okeechobee 304 NW 2nd St. Okeechobee, FL 33472 813-763-3421	Orange 46 E. Robinson St. Orlando, FL 32801 407-836-2700
Osceola 12 S. Vernon St. Kissimmee, FL 32741 407-847-1421	Palm Beach 301 N. Olive West Palm Beach, FL 33401 561-355-2264
Paseo 705 E. Live Oak Ave. Dade City, FL 38053 904-521-4408	Pinellas 315 Court St. Clearwater, FL 34616 813-363-3561
Putman 410 St. James Ave. Palatka, FL 32078 904-329-0272	Saint Johns 244 S. Matanzas Blvd St. Augustine, FL 32085 904-823-2250
Saint Lucie 221 S. Indian River Dr. Ft. Pierce, FL 33450 407-462-1650	Santa Rosa 801 Caroline SE Milton, FL 32570 904-623-0135
Sarasota 2000 Main St. Sarasota, FL 34237 813-951-5620	Seminole 300 North Park Ave. Sanford, FL 32771 407-321-1130
Sumter 209 N. Florida St. Bushnell, FL 33513 904-793-0260	Suwannee 200 South Ohio Ave. Live Oak, FL 32060 904-364-3440

Taylor	Union
108 N. Jefferson	55 Main St. W
Perry, FL 32347	Lake Butler, FL 32054
904-838-3517	904-496-3331
Volusia	Wakulla
120 W Indiana Ave.	202 Oklochnee St.
Deland, FL 32720	Crawfordville, FL 32326
904-736-5939	904-926-3371
Walton	Washington
100 East Nelson	203 W. Cypress
DeFuniak Springs, FL 32434	Chipley, FL 32428
904-898-8121	904-638-6276

Illinois

Illinois has a statutory penalty interest rate of 18% that occurs every six months, but in some cases the interest rate can be higher than 18%. The successful bidder is the one willing to accept the lowest rate of interest. The redemption period is 2 ½ years each county varies. Please note, sales dates vary by county.

Alexander County	Bond County
County Courthouse	County Courthouse
2000 Washington Avenue	200 W College
Cairo, IL 62914-1717	Greenville, IL 62246-0407
618-734-0386	618-664-1966
Boone County	Brown County
County Courthouse	County Courthouse
601 North Main St.	1 Court St, Room 4
Belvidere, IL 61008-2708	Mount Sterling, IL 62353-0142
815-547-4770	217-773-3421
Bureau County	Calhoun County
County Courthouse	County Courthouse
700 S. Main St.	PO Box 187
Princeton, IL 61356-0366	Hardin, IL 62047-0187
815-875-2014	618-576-2351

Cass County County Courthouse 100 East Springfield St. Virginia, IL 62691 217-452-7217	Champaign County County Courthouse 101 E. Main Urbana, IL 61801 217-384-3772
Clark County Christian County County Courthouse PO Box 647 Taylorville, IL 217-824-4969	Clay County County Courthouse PO Box 160 Louisville, IL 62858-0160 618-665-3626
Clinton County County Courthouse PO Box 308 Carlyle, IL 62231 618-594-2464	Crawford County County Courthouse PO Box 602 Robinson, IL 62454-0602 618-546-1212
Cumberland County County Courthouse PO Box 146 Toledo, IL 62468-0146 217-849-2631	DeWitt County County Courthouse PO Box 439 Clinton, IL 61727-0439 217-935-2119
Douglas County County Courthouse PO Box 467 Tuscola, IL 61953 217-253-2411	Edger County County Courthouse 115 West Court St. Paris, IL 61944 217-466-7433
Edwards County County Courthouse 50 E. Main St. Albion, IL 62806 618-445-2115	Fayette County County Courthouse PO Box 5004 Vandalia, IL 62471 618-283-5000
Franklin County County Courthouse PO Box 607 Benton, IL 62812 618-438-3221	Fulton County County Courthouse PO Box 226 Lewistown, IL 61542 309-547-3041

Gallatin County County Courthouse PO Box 550 Shawneetown, IL 62984-0550 618-269-3025	Greene County County Courthouse 519 North Main Carrollton, IL 62016 217-942-5443
Grundy County County Administration Center 1320 Union St. Morris, IL 60450 815-941-3400	Hamilton County County Courthouse McLeansboro, IL 62859 618-643-2721
Hancock County County Courthouse PO Box 39 Carthage, IL 62321-0039	Hardin County County Courthouse PO Box 187 Elizabethtown, IL 62931 618-287-2251
Henderson County County Courthouse PO Box 308 Oquawka, IL 61469-0308 309-867-2911	Jasper County County Courthouse 100 West Jordan St. Newton, IL 62448-1973 618-783-3124
Jefferson County County Courthouse Mount Vernon, IL 62864 618-244-8000	Jo Davies County County Courthouse 330 North Bench St. Galena, IL 61036 815-777-0161
Jersey County County Courthouse 102 West Pearl St Jerseyville, IL 62052-1675 618-498-5571	Johnson County County Courthouse PO Box 96 Vienna, IL 62995-0096 618-658-3611
Knox County County Courthouse 200 South Cherry St Galesburg, IL 61401-4912 309-343-3121	Kendall County County Office Building 111 W Fox St. Yorkville, IL 60560-1675

Lawrence County County Courthouse 1100 State St. Lawrence, IL 62439 618-943-2346	LaSalle County County Courthouse 707 E Etna Road Ottawa, IL 61350-1047 815-434-8200
Macoupin County County Courthouse PO Box 39 Carlinville, IL 62626-0039 217-854-3214	Livingston County County Courthouse 112 W Madison St. Pontiac, IL 61764 815-844-2006
Marshall County County Courthouse P.O Box 328 Lacon, IL 61540-0328 309-246-6325	Marion County County Courthouse PO Box 637 Salem, IL 62881-0637 618-548-3400
Massac County County Courthouse PO Box 429 Metropolis, IL 62960-0429 618-524-5213	Mason County County Courthouse P.O Box 77 Havana, IL 62644-0077 309-543-6661
Menard County County Courthouse PO Box 456 Petersburg, IL 62675-0456 217-632-2415	McDonough County County Courthouse 1 Courthouse Square Macomb, IL 61455 309-837-2308
Monroe County County Courthouse 100 S Main St. Waterloo, IL 62298-1322 618-939-8681	Mercer County County Courthouse 100 SE 3rd St. Aledo, IL 61231 309-582-7021
Morgan County County Courthouse 300 W State St Jacksonville, IL 62650-2083 217-245-4619	Montgomery County County Courthouse 1 Courthouse Square Hillsboro, IL 62049 217-532-9530

Perry County County Courthouse PO Box 438 Route 127 S. Pinckneyville, IL 62274-0438 618-357-5116	Moultrie County County Courthouse 10 South Main St. Sullivan, IL 61951 217-728-4389
Pope County County Courthouse 400 Main St Golconda, IL 62938 618-683-4466	Pulaski County County Courthouse PO Box 318 Mound City, IL 62963-0218 618-748-9360
Putnam County County Courthouse PO Box 13 Hennepin, IL 61327 815-925-7129	Randolph County County Courthouse 1 Taylor Street Chester, IL 62233 618-826-2510
Richland County County Courthouse 103 W. Main Olney, IL 62450 618-392-3111	Saline County County Courthouse 10 East Poplar St Harrisburg, IL 62946 618-252-6905
Schuyler County County Courthouse Rural Route 1, PO Box 43E Rushville, IL 62681 217-322-4734	Scott County County Courthouse 23 East Market St. Winchester, IL 62694 217-742-3178
Shelby County County Courthouse PO Box 230 Shelbyville, IL 62565 217-774-4421	St. Clair County County Courthouse 10 Public Square Belleville, IL 62220-1623 618-277-6600
Stark County County Courthouse PO Box 97 Toulon, IL 61483-0097 309-286-5911	Stephenson County County Courthouse 15 North Galena Avenue Freeport, IL 61032-4348 815-235-8289

Tazewell County	Union County
McKenzie Building	County Courthouse
Fourth And Court Streets	PO Box H
Pekin, IL 61554	Jonesboro, IL 62952-0478
309-477-2272	618-833-5711
Wabash County	Warren County
County Courthouse	County Courthouse
PO Box 277	100 W. Broadway
Mount Carmel, IL 62863-0277	Monmouth, IL 61462
618-262-4561	309-734-8592
Washington County	Wayne County
County Courthouse	County Courthouse
101 E St. Louis St.	PO Box 187
Nashville, IL 62263	Fairfield, IL 62837-0187
618-327-8314	618-842-5182
White County	Williamson County
County Courthouse	County Courthouse
PO Box 339	200 West Jefferson
Carmi, IL 62821-0339	Marion, IL 62959-3061
618-382-7211	618-997-1301
Winnebago County	Woodford County
County Courthouse	County Courthouse
404 Elm St.	115 N. Main St, Suite 202
Rockford, IL 61101-1212	Eureka, IL 61530-1274
815-987-2590	309-467-2822

Indiana

Adams County	Bartholomew County
County Courthouse	County Courthouse
112 South Second	440 3rd St.
Decatur, IN 46733-1618	Columbus, IN 47201
(219)724-2600	

Benton County County Courthouse 706 East 5th Street Fowler, IN 47944-1556 (765) 884-0930	Blackford County County Courthouse 110 West Washington Hartford City, IN 47348 (765)348-1620
Boone County 201 Courthouse Square Lebanon, IN 46052-2126 (765) 482-2940	Brown County P.O Box 37 Nashville, IN 47448-0037 (812) 988-5485
Carrol County P.O Box 28 Delphi, IN 46923-0028 (317) 564-3172	Cass County 200 Court Park Logansport, IN 46947 (219) 753-7720
Clark County City-County Bldg, 501 E. Court Jeffersonville, IN 47130 (812)283-4451	Clinton County 125 Courthouse Square Frankfort, IN 46041 (765) 659-6330
Crawford P.O Box 316 English, IN 47118 (812) 338-2601	Daviess County 200 East Walnut Washington, IN 47501 (812) 254-8662
Dearborn County County Administrator Bldg. 215 West High Street Lawrenceburg, IN 47025-1662 (812) 537-8824	Dekalb County County Courthouse 100 South Main Street Auburn, IN 46706 (219) 925-2362
Delaware County County Courthouse 100 West Main Street Muncie, IN 47305 (765) 747-7726	Dubois 1 Courthouse Square Jasper, IN 47546 (812) 481-7000
Fayette County County Courthouse 401 Central Avenue Connersville, IN 47331-1903 (765) 825-8987	Floyd County City County Building 311 West 1st New Albany, IN 47150 (812) 948-5446

Fountain County 301 4th Street Covington, IN 47932 (765)793-2243	Franklin County / County Courthouse 459 Main Street Brookville, IN 47012-1405 (765) 647-4613
Fulton County 815 Main Street Rochester, IN 46975-1546 (219) 223-2912	Gibson County / County Courthouse 101 N. Main Princeton, IN 47670-0168 (812) 385-4927
Grant County County Courthouse Marion, IN 46953 (765) 668-8871	Greene County County Courthouse Bloomfield, IN 47424 (812) 384-8532
Hamilton County County Courthouse One Hamilton County Square Noblesville, IN 46060 (317) 776-9601	Hancock County County Courthouse 9 E. Main, Room 208 Greenfield, IN 46140 (317) 462-1106
Harrison County County Courthouse 300 N. Capitol Ave. Corydon, IN 47112 (812) 738-8241	Hendricks County P.O Box 599 Danville, IN 46113-0188 (317) 745-9221
Henry County County Courthouse 101 S. Main New Castle, IN 47362 (765) 529-6401	Howard County 117 N. Main Kokomo, IN 46901 (765) 456-2216
Huntington County County Courthouse 201 N. Jefferson, Room 103 Huntington, IN 46750 (219) 358-4822	Jackson County P.O Box 122 Brownstown, IN 47220 (812) 358-6116
Jasper County /County Courthouse Box 5 Rensselaer, IN 47978 (219) 866-4930	Jay County / County Courthouse 120 Court Street Portland, IN 47371 (219) 726-7575

Jefferson County County Courthouse 300 E. Main Street Madison, IN 47250-3537	Jennings County P.O Box 383 Vernon, IN 47282 (812)346-2131
Johnson County 5 West Jefferson Franklin, IN 46131 (317)736-5000	Knox County Vincennes, IN 47591-2002 (812) 885-2502
La Porte County 813 Lincoln Way La Porte, IN 46350 (219) 326-6808	LaGrange County 105 North Detroit Street LaGrange, IN 46761 (219) 463-3442
Lake County 2293 N. Main Street Crown Point, IN 46307-1854 (219) 755-3200	Madison County 16 E. 9th Street Anderson, IN 46016-1538 (765) 641-9470
Marion County 2500 City County Building Indianapolis, IN 46204 (317)236-3200	Marshall County 112 W. Jefferson Street Plymouth, IN 46563 (219) 935-8555
Martin County P.O Box 600 Shoals, IN 47581-0600 (812) 247-3731	Miami County P.O Box 184 Peru, IN 46970-2231 (765) 472-3901
Monroe County County Courthouse Bloomington, IN 47402-0547 (812) 349-2550	Montgomery County P.O Box 768 Crawfordsville, IN 47933-0768 (765) 364-6430
Morgan County 180 S. Main St. Martinsville, IN 46151 (765) 342-1001	Newton County 201 North Third Street Kentland, IN 47951-0143 (219) 474-6081
Noble County / County Courthouse 101 North Orange Street Albion, IN 46701-1049 (219) 636-2658	Ohio County 413 Main St. Rising Sun, IN 47040 (812) 438-2062

Orange County 205 E. Main Street Paoli, IN 47454 (812) 723-2649	Owen County 60 S. Main Spencer, IN 47460 (812) 829-5000
Parke County 116 West High Street Rockville, IN 47872-1716 (765) 569-3422	Perry County / County Courthouse 2219 Payne Street Tell City, IN 47586-2830 (812) 547-6427
Pike County 801 Main Street Petersburg, IN 47567 (812) 354-8448	Porter County 155 Indiana Avenue Val Paraiso, IN 46383 (219) 465-3332
Posey County P.O Box 745 Mount Vernon, IN 47620-0745 (812) 838-1300	Pulaski County 112 E. Main Winamac, IN 46996 (219) 946-3653
Putnam County 1 West Washington Street Greencastle, IN 46135 (765) 653-4603	Randolph County 100 South Main Street Winchester, IN 47394 (765) 584-7070
Ripley County PO Box 235 Versailles, IN 47042 (812) 689-6115	Rush County 101 East 2nd Street Rushville, IN 46173-1854 (765) 932-2077
Scott County 1 E. McClain Ave. Scottsburg, IN 47170-1662 (812) 752-8408	Shelby County 407 S. Harrison Street Shelbyville, IN 46176 (317) 392-6330
Spencer County 200 Main St. Rockport, IN 47635-0012 (812) 649-4376	St. Joseph County 101 South Main Street South Bend, IN 46601 (219) 235-9534
Starke County / County Courthouse 53 E. Mound Street Knox, IN 46534 (219) 772-9101	Steuben County / County Courthouse 55 S. Public Service Angola, IN 46703 (219) 668-1000

Sullivan County / County Courthouse P.O Box 370 Sullivan, IN 47882-0370 (812) 268-4491	Switzerland County /County Courthouse 212 West Main Street Vevay, IN 47043 (812) 427-3302
Tippecanoe County County Courthouse 301 Main Street Lafayette, IN 47901-1211 (765) 423-9326	Tipton County County Courthouse 101 East Jefferson Tipton, IN 46072 (765) 675-2794
Vanderburgh County County Courthouse 825 Sycamore Street Evansville, IN 47708-1831 (812) 435-5241	Vermillion County County Courthouse P.O Box 190 Newport, IN 47966-0190 (765) 492-3570
Vigo County Third and Wabash Terre Haute, IN 47807 (812) 462-3367	Wabash County / County Courthouse 1 W. Hill Street Wabash, IN 46992 (219) 563-0661
Warren County / County Courthouse 125 N. Monroe Street Williamsport, IN 47993-1198 (765) 762-3275	Warrick County / County Courthouse 109 W. Main Street Boonville, IN 47601 (812) 897-6120
Washington County / County Courthouse 99 Public Square Salem, IN 47167 (812)-883-4805	Wayne County 301 East Main Street Richmond, IN 47374 (765) 973-9200
Wells County 105 W. Market Square, Suite 205 Bluffton, IN 46714 (219) 824-6470	White County P.O Box 260 Monticello, IN 47960 (219) 583-5761
Whitley County County Courthouse 101 W Van Buren Columbia City, IN 46725 (219) 248-3100	

Iowa

Adair County 400 Public Square Greenfield, IA 50849-1259 (641)743-2445	Adams County P.O Box 28 Corning, IA 50841 (515) 322-3340
Allamakee County 110 Allamakee Street Waukon, IA 52172-1747 (563) 568-3522	Benton County P.O Box 549 Vinton, IA 52349-0719 (319) 472-2365
Boone County 201 State Street Boone, IA 50036 (515) 433-0502	Buchanan County P.O Box 317 Independence, IA 50644-0317 (319) 334-2196
Buena Vista County P.O Box 220 Storm Lake, IA 50588-0220 (712) 749-2542	Butler County P.O Box 325 Allison, IA 50602-0325 (319) 267-2670
Calhoun County 416 4th Street Rockwell City, IA 50579 (712) 297-7741	Carroll County P.O Box 867 Carroll, IA 51401-0867 (712) 792-4923
Cass County 5 W. 7th Street Atlantic, IA 50022-1492 (712) 243-4570	Cedar County 400 Cedar Street Tipton, IA 52772-1750 (319) 886-3168
Cerro Gordo County 220 North Washington Mason City, IA 50401-3254 (641) 421-3021	Cherokee County 520 West Main St. Cherokee, IA 51012 (712) 225-6704
Chickasaw County P.O Box 311 New Hampton, IA 50659-0311 (641) 394-2100	Clarke County 100 South Main St. Osceola, IA 50213 (614) 342-3311

Clay County 215 West 4th St. Spencer, IA 51301-3822 (712) 262-1569	Clayton County P.O Box 416 Elkader, IA 52043-0416 (563) 245-2533
Clinton County County Administration Building 1900 North 3rd ST Clinton, IA 52733 (563) 244-0560	Crawford County 1202 Broadway Denison, IA 51442-0423 (712) 263-3045
Dallas County 801 Court St. Adel, IA 50003-1476 (515) 993-5816	Davis County Courthouse Square Bloomfield, IA 52537 (515) 664-2344
Decatur County 207 North Main Leon, IA 50144 (641) 446-4382	Delaware County 301 East Main Manchester, IA 52057 (319) 927-2515
Dickinson County 1802 Hill Ave. Spirit Lake, IA 51360-1259 (712) 336-3356	Dubuque County 720 Central Dubuque, IA 52001 (319) 589-4441
Emmet County 609 1st Ave. North Estherville, IA 51334 (712) 362-4261	Fayette County P.O Box 267 West Union, IA 52175-0267 (319) 422-3497
Floyd County 101 South Main St. Charles City, IA 50616-2756 (641) 257-6131	Franklin County P.O Box 26 Hampton, IA 50441-0026 (641) 456-5622
Fremont County P.O Box 610 Sidney, IA 51652-0610 (712) 374-2415	Greene County 114 N. Chestnut Jefferson, IA 50129 (515) 386-2316
Grundy County 706 G Avenue Grundy Center, IA 50638 (319) 824-3122	Guthrie County 200 North Fifth Street, Guthrie Center, IA 50115 (515) 747-3512

Hamilton County 2300 Superior Street, Suite 9 Webster City, IA 50595 (515) 832-9530	Hancock County 855 State St. Garner, IA 50438-1637 (641) 923-3163
Hardin County 1215 Edgington Ave. Eldora, IA 50627 (641) 858-3461	Harrison County 111 North 2nd Ave. Logan, IA 51546 (712) 644-2401
Henry County P.O Box 149 Mount Pleasant, IA 52641-0149 (319) 385-0759	Howard County 137 North Elm Cresco, IA 51236-1526 (319) 547- 2880
Humboldt County 203 Main St. P.O Box 100 Dakota City, IA 50529-0100 (515) 332-1571	Ida County 401 Moore Head St. Ida Grove, IA 51445-1429 (712) 364-2626
Iowa County P.O Box 126 Marengo, IA 52301-0126 (319) 642-3923	Jackson County 201 West Platt Maquoketa, IA 52060-2295 (563) 652-3144
Jasper County P.O Box 944 Newton, IA 50208 (641) 792-7016	Jefferson County P.O Box 984 Fairfield, IA 52556-0984 (641) 472-2851
Johnson County County Administrative Building 913 S. Dubuque Iowa City, IA 52244 (319) 356-6000	Jones County P.O Box 109 Anamosa, IA 52205 (319)-462-2282
Keokuk County 101 S. Main St. Sigourney, IA 52591-1499 (641) 622-2320	Lee County 933 Ave H P.O Box 190 Fort Madison, IA 52627 (319) 372-6557
Louisa County 117 South Main Wapello, IA 52653 (319) 523-3371	Lucas County 916 Braden Ave. Chariton, IA 50049-1825 (515) 774-2018

Lyon County 206 S. 2nd Avenue Rock Rapids, IA 51246 (712) 472-3713	Madison County P.O Box 152 Winterset, IA 50273-0152 (515) 462-3225
Mahaska County 106 South 1st St. Oskaloosa, IA 52577 (641) 673-3469	Marion County P.O Box 497 Knoxville, IA 50138-0497 (515) 828-2231
Marshall County 17 East Main Street Marshalltown, IA 50158 641-754-6330	Mills County 418 Sharp Street Glenwood, IA 51534 712-527-3146
Mitchell County 508 State St. Osage, IA 50461 (515) 732-5861	Monona County 610 Iowa Avenue Onawa, IA 51040-1660 712-423-1585
Monroe County 10 Benton Avenue East Albia, IA 52531 515-932-7706	Montgomery County PO Box 469 Red Oak, IA 51566 712-623-5127
Muscatine County 401 East Third Street Muscatine, IA 52761-4168 319-263-5317	O` Brien County P.O. Box M Primghar, IA 51245 712-757-3255
Osceola County 300 Seventh Street, Suite 6 Sibley, IA 51249-1648 712-754-2241	Page County 112 East Main St Clarinda, IA 51632 712-542-3219
Palo Alto County 1010 Broadway, Emmetsburg, IA 50536 712-852-2924	Plymouth County 215 Fourth Avenue SE, LeMars, IA 51031-2194 712-546-6100
Pocahontas County 99 Court Square, Pocahontas, IA 50574 712-335-3361	Polk County Court Administrative Office Bldg. 111 Court Ave. Des Moines, IA 50309-2218 512-286-3117

Pottawattamie County 227 S. 6th Street Council Bluffs, IA 51501-4208 712-328-5604	Poweshiek County P.O. Box 57 Montezuma, IA 50171 641-623-5443
Scott County 400 West Fourth Street Davenport, IA 52801 563-326-8611	Shelby County 612 Court Street Harlan, IA 51537 712-755-3831
Sioux County P.O. Box 18 SW Orange City, IA 51041-0018 712-737-2286	Story County 9006th St Nevada, IA 50201 515-382-7200
Tama County 100 West High Street Toledo, IA 52342 515-484-3980	Taylor County 405 Jefferson Street Bedford, IA 50833 712-523-2280
Union County 300 North Pine Creston, IA 50801 515-782-7918	Van Buren County PO Box 475 Keosauqua, IA 52565 319-293-3129
Wapello County 101 West Fourth Street Ottumwa, IA 52501 641-683-0020	Warren County 301 North Buxton, Suite 202 Indianola, IA 50125 515-961-1028
Wayne County PO Box 435 Corydon, IA 50060 641-872-2264	Webster County 703 Central Avenue Fort Dodge, IA 50501 515-573-7175
Winnebago County 126 South Clark St Forest City, IA 50436 641-582-3412	Winneshiek County 201 West Main Street Decorah, IA 52101-1713 319-382-5085
Woodbury County 620 Douglas St Sioux City, IA 51101-1248 712-279-6525	Worth County 1000 Central Ave Northwood, IA 50459 319-324-2316

| Wright County
115 North Main Street
Clarion, IA 50525
515-532-3113 | |

Kentucky

Adair County 424 Public Sq. Ste. 1 Columbia, KY 42728 (270) 237-3631	Bath County P.O. Box 39 Owingsville, KY 40360 (606) 674-6346
Boone County 2950 Washington Street Burlington, KY 41005 (606) 334-2100	Boyd County P.O. Box 423 Catlettsburg, KY 41129 (606) 739-4134
Bracken County P.O. Box 264 Brooksville, KY 41004 (606) 735-2300	Breckinridge County P.O. Box 227 Hardinsburg, KY 40143 (270) 756-2269
Butler County P.O. Box 626 Morgantown, KY 42261 (270) 526-3433	Calloway County 101 South 5th Street Murray, KY 42071 (270) 753-2920
Carlisle County P.O Box 279 Bardwell, KY 42023 (270) 628-3233	Christian County 511 South Main Street Hopkinsville, KY 42240 (270) 887-4100
Clay County 316 Main St. Suite 129 Manchester, KY 40962 (606) 598-2071	Crittenden County 107 S. Main Street Marion, KY 42064 (270) 965-5251
Daviess County 212 St. Ann Street Owensboro, KY 42303 (270) 685-8424	Elliott County P.O. Box 710 Sandy Hook, KY 41171 (606) 738-5421

Fayette County 200 E. Main St. Lexington, KY 40507 (859) 258-3000	Floyd County P.O Box 1089 Prestonsburg, KY 41653 (606) 886-9193
Fulton County 2204 S. 7th Street Hickman, KY 42050 (270) 236-2594	Garrard County 15 Public Square Lancaster, KY 40444 (606) 792-3531
Graves County 201 East College St. Mayfield, KY 42066 (270) 247-1733	Green County 203 W. Court Street Greensburg, KY 42743 (270) 932-5386
Hancock County P.O. Box 580 Hawesville, KY 42348 (270) 927-8137	Harlan County P.O. Box 670 Harlan, KY 40831 (606) 573-2600
Hart County P.O. Box 490 Munfordville, KY 42765 (270) 524-5219	Henry County P.O. Box 202 New Castle, KY 40050 (502) 845-5707
Hopkins County 10 South Main St. Madisonville, KY 42431 (270) 821-7361	Jefferson County Louisville, KY 40204 (502) 574-2273
Johnson County P.O. Box 868 Paintsville, KY 41240 (606) 789-2550	Knott County P.O. Box 1287 Hindman, KY 41822 (606) 785-5592
Larue County 209 W. High Hodgenville, KY 42748 (270) 358-4400	Lawrence County 122 S. Main Cross St. Louisa, KY 41230 (606) 638-4102
Leslie County P.O. Box 619 Hyden, KY 41749 (606) 672-3200	Lewis County 514 2nd Avenue Vanceburg, KY 41179 (606) 796-2722

Livingston County	Lyon County
P.O. Box 70	PO Box 698
Smithland, KY 42081	Eddyville, KY 42038
(270) 928-2106	(270) 388-7311
Magoffin County	Marshall County
P.O. Box 430	1101 Main Street
Salyersville, KY 41465	Benton, KY 42025
(606) 349-2313	(270) 527-4750
Mason County	McCreary County
219 Stanley Reed Court	PO Box 579
Maysville, KY 41056	Whitely City, KY 42653
(606) 564-6706	(606) 376-2413
Meade County	Mercer County
516 Fairway Drive	134 South Main
Brandenburg, KY 40108	Harrodsburg, KY 40330
(270) 422-3967	(606) 734-6310
Monroe County	Morgan County
P.O. Box 305	450 Prestonsburg St
Tompkinsville, KY 42167	West Liberty, KY 41472
(270) 487-5505	(606) 743-3949
Nelson County	Ohio County
113 E. Stephen Foster Ave.	P.O. Box 146
Bardstown, KY 40004	Hartford, KY 42347
(502) 348-1820	(270) 298-4400
Owen County	Pendleton County
P.O Box 465	233 Main Street, Rm. 4
Owenton, KY 40359	Falmouth, KY 41040
(502) 484-3405	(859) 654-4321
Pike County	Pulaski County
Pikeville, KY 41501	P.O. Box 712
(606)432-6247	Somerset, KY 42502
	(606) 678-4853
Russell County	Shelby County
P.O. Box 397	501 Main St.
Jamestown, KY 42629	Shelbyville, KY 40065
(270) 343-2112	(502) 633-1220

Spencer County P.O. Box 397 Taylorsville, KY 40071 (502) 477-3205	Todd County P.O. Box 355 Elkton, KY 42220 (270) 265-2363
Trimble County P.O. Box 251 Bedford, KY 40006 (502) 255-7196	Warren County 429 E. 10th Street Bowling Green, KY 42101 (270) 842-9416
Wayne County 109 Main St. Monticello, KY 42633 (606) 348-4241	Whitley County P.O. Box 237 Williamsburg, KY 40769 (606) 549-6002
Woodford County 103 S. Main St., Ste.200 Versailles, KY 40383 (859) 873-4139	

Maryland

Allegany County 701 Kelly Road, Suite 405 Cumberland, MD 21502 301-777-5911	Anne Arundel County 8 Church Circle Annapolis, MD 21401 410-222-7000
Baltimore County 400 Washington Ave. Townson, MD 21204 410-887-3196	Calvert County 175 Main St. Prince Frederick, MD 20678-3337 410-535-1600
Carrol County 225 North Center St. Westminster, MD 21157-5194 410-386-2400	Cecil County 129 East Main St. Elkton, MD 21921 410-996-5201
Carolina County 109 Market St. RM 109 Denton, MD 21629 410-479-0660	City of Baltimore / City Hall 100 North Holiday St. Baltimore, MD 21202 410-396-4892

Dorchester County 206 S. High St. Cambridge, MD 21613-0026 410-228-6300	Frederick County /Winchester Hall 12 E. Church St. Frederick, MD 21701 301-694-1100
Garrett County 203 South Fourth St. Oakland, MD 21550-1535 301-334-8970	Harford County 20 West Courtland St. Bel Air, MD 21014-3745 410-638-3343
Howard County 3430 Courthouse Drive Ellicott City, MD 21043 410-313-2011	Kent County 103 North Cross St Chestertown, MD 21620 410-778-7435
Montgomery County 50 Maryland Ave Rockville, MD 20850-2540 301-217-7778	Prince George`s County 14741 Governor Oden Bowie Dr. 3200 Upper Marlboro, MD 20772-3050 301-952-4131
Queen Anne`s County 107 N. Liberty St. Centreville, MD 21617 410-758-1773	Somerset County P.O Box 37 Princess Anne, MD 21853-0037 410-651-0320
St. Mary`s County P.O Box 653 Leonardtown, MD 20650-0653 301-475-4461	Talbot County County Courthouse 11 North Washington St. Easton, MD 21601 410-770-8001
Washington County County Courthouse Annex 100 W. Washington St. Hagerstown, MD 21740 301-791-3090	Wicomico County P.O. Box 870 Salisbury, MD 21803-0870 410-548-4801
Worcester County County Courthouse 1 West Market St. Snow Hill, MD 21863-1072 410-632-1194	

Mississippi

Adams County P.O Box 1008 Natchez, MS 39121-1008 601-442-2431	Alcorn County P.O Box 69 Corinth, MS 38834-0069 662-286-7700
Amite County P.O Box 680 Liberty, MS 39645 601-657-8022	Benton County P.O Box 218 Ashland, MS 38603-0218 662-224-6611
Bolivar County P.O Box 698 Cleveland, MS 38732 662-843-2071	Calhoun County P.O Box 8 Pittsboro, MS 38951-0008 662-983-3117
Carroll County 1 Pinson Square Carrollton, MS 38917 601-237-9274	Chickasaw County 101 North Jefferson St. Houston, MS 38851 662-456-2513
Choctaw County P.O Box 250 Ackerman, MS 39735-0250 662-285-6329	Claiborne County 410 Main St. Port Gibson, MS 39150 601-437-4992
Clarke County P.O Box 616 Quitman, MS 39355-0815 601-776--3567	Clay County P.O Box 815 WestPoint, MS 39773-0815 662-494-3124
Copiah County P.O Box 551 Hazlehurst, MS 39083 601-892-2994	Covington County P.O Box 1679 Collins, MS 39428-1679 601-765-8605
Desoto County 2535 Highway 51 S. Hernando, MS 38632-2132 662-429-1460	Franklin County P.O Box 297 Meadville, MS 39653-0297 601-384-2330

George County	Greene County
355 Cox St., Suite D	P.O Box 460
Lucedale, MS 39452	Leakesville, MS 39451
601-947-7506	601-394-2394
Grenada County	Hancock County
P.O Box 1208	P.O Box 429
Grenada, MS 38902-1208	Bay Saint Louis, MS 39520
662-226-1821	228-467-0172
Harrison County	Hinds County
P.O Box CC	P.O Box 686
Gulfport, MS 39502-0860	Jackson, MS 39205-0686
228-865-4001	601-968-6501
Holmes County	Humphrey`s County
P.O Box 239	P.O Box 547
Lexington, MS 39095-0239	Belzoni, MS 39038-0547
602-834-2508	662-247-1740
Issaquena County	Itawamba County
P.O Box 27	P.O Box 776
Mayersville, MS 39113	Fulton, MS 38843
662-873-2761	662-862-3421
Jackson County	Jasper County
P.O Box 998	P.O Box 1047
Pascagoula, MS 39568-0998	Bay Springs, MS 39422-1047
228-769-3100	601-764-3368
Jefferson County	Jefferson Davis County
P.O Box 145	P.O Box 1137
Fayette, MS 39069-0145	Prentiss, MS 39474-1137
601-786-3021	601-792-4204
Jones County	Kemper County
P.O Box 1468	P.O Box 188
Laurel, MS 39441-1468	DeKalb, MS 39328-0188
601-428-3139	601-743-2460

Lafayette County P.O Box 1240 Oxford, MS 38655-1240 662-234-2131	Lauderdale County P.O Box 1587 Meridian, MS 39302-1587 601-482-9746
Lawrence County P.O Box 1160 Monticello, MS 39654 601-587-7162	Leake County P.O Drawer 72 Carthage, MS 39051-00072 601-267-8002
Lee County P.O Box 1785 Tupelo, MS 38801-1785 662-841-9110	Leflore County P.O Box 250 Greenwood, MS 38935-0250 662-455-3904
Lincoln County P.O Box 555 Brookhaven, MS 39601-0555 601-835-3479	Madison County P.O Box 404 Canton, MS 39046-0404 601-859-1177
Marion County 250 Board St. Suite 2 Columbia, MS 39429 601-736-2691	Marshall County P.O Box 219 Holly Springs, MS 38635 662-252-4431
Monroe County P.O Box 578 Aberdeen, MS 39730-0578 662-369-8143	Montgomery County P.O Box 71 Winona, MS 38967-0071 662-283-2333
Neshoba County 401 Beacone St. Philadelphia, MS 39350 601-656-6281	Newton County P.O Box 68 Decatur, MS 39327-0068 601-635-2367
Noxubee County P.O Box 147 Macon, MS 39341 662-726-4243	Oktibbeha County 101 East Main St. Starkville, MS 39759 662-323-5834
Panola County 151 Public Square Batesville, MS 38606 662-563-6201	Pearl River County P.O Box 431 Poplarville, MS 39470-0431 601-795-2237

Perry County P.O Box 198 New Augusta, MS 39462-0198 601-964-8398	Pike County 218 East Bay St, P.O Box 431 Magnolia, MS 39652 601-783-5289
Pontotoc County P.O Box 209 Pontotoc, MS 38863-0209 662-489-3900	Quitman County 230 Chestnut St. Marks, MS 38646 662-326-2661
Rankin County 305 Government St. Brandon, MS 39042 601-825-1475	Scott County P.O Box 630 Forest, MS 39074-0630 601-469-1926
Sharkey County P.O Box 218 Rolling Fork, MS 39159-0218 662-873-2755	Simpson County P.O Box 367 Mendenhall, MS 39114-0367 601-847-1418
Stone County P.O Drawer 7 Wiggins, MS 39577 601-928-5266	Sunflower County P.O Box 988 Indianola, MS 38751-0988 662-887-4703
Tallahatchie County P.O Box 350 Charleston, MS 38921 662-647-5551	Tate County 201 S. Ward St Senatobia, MS 38668-2616 662-562-5661
Tippah County P.O Box 99 Ripley, MS 38663-0099 662-837-7374	Tishomingo County 1008 Battleground Drive Iuka, MS 38852 662-423-7032
Tunica County P.O Box 639 Tunica, MS 38676-0639 662-363-1465	Union County P.O Box 847 New Albany, MS 38652-0847 662-534-5284
Walthall County P.O Box 351 Tylertown, MS 39667-0351 601-876-3553	Warren County P.O Box 351 Vicksburg, MS 39181-0351 601-636-4415

Washington County P.O Box 309 Greenville, MS 38702-0309 662-378-8355	Wayne County 609 Azalea Drive Waynesboro, MS 39367-1249 662-735-2873
Webster County P.O Box 398 Walthall, MS 39771 662-258-4131	Wilkinson County P.O Box 1284 Woodville, MS 39669-0516 601-888-4381
Winston County P.O Drawer 69 Louisville, MS 39339 662-773-3631	Yalobusha County P.O Box 664 Water Valley, MS 38965-0664 662-473-2091
Yazoo County P.O Box 1106 Yazoo City, MS 39194-0068 662-746-2661	

Missouri

Adair County County Courthouse 106 North Washington St. Kirksville, MO 63501 660-665-3350	Andrew County County Courthouse P.O Box 206 Savannah, MO 64485 816-324-3624
Atchison County County Courthouse P.O Box 280 Rockport, MO 64482 660-774-6214	Barry County County Courthouse 700 Main St. Suite 2 Cassville, MO 65625 417-847-2561
Barton County County Courthouse 1004 Gulf Lamar, MO 64759 417-682-3529	Bates County County Courthouse 1 North Delaware St. Butler, MO 64730 660-679-3371

Benton County County Courthouse P.O Box 1238 Warsaw, MO 65355-1238 660-438-7406	Bollinger County County Courthouse P.O Box 110 Marble Hill, MO 63764 573-238-2126
Butler County County Courthouse 105 Main St. Poplar Bluff, MO 63901 573-686-8050	Caldwell County County Courthouse P.O Box 67 Kingston, MO 64650-0067 816-586-2571
Callaway County County Courthouse 10 East 5th St. Fulton, MO 65251 573-642-0780	Camden County County Courthouse 1 Court Circle Camdenton, MO 65020 573-346-4440
Carroll County County Courthouse City Square Carrollton, MO 64633 660-542-0615	Carter County County Courthouse P.O Box 517 Van Buren, MO 63965-0517 573-323-4527
Cedar County County Courthouse P.O Box 126 Stockton, MO 65785-0126	Chariton County County Courthouse 306 S. Cherry Keytesville, MO 65261 660-288-3273
Christian County County Courthouse 100 West Church Ozark, MO 65721-0549 417-581-6360	Clark County County Courthouse 111 East Court St. Kahoka, MO 63445 660-727-3283
Clay County County Courthouse Courthouse Square Liberty, MO 64068 816-792-7733	Clinton County County Courthouse P.O Box 245 Plattsburgh, MO 64477-0245 816-539-3713

Cole County County Courthouse 301 East High Jefferson City, MO 65101 573-634-9100	Cooper County County Courthouse 200 Main St. Boonville, MO 65233-1276 660-882-2114
Crawford County County Courthouse P.O Box AS Steelville, MO 65565-0620 573-775-2376	Dade County County Courthouse Main St. Greenfield, MO 65661 417-637-2724
Dallas County County Courthouse P.O Box 436 Buffalo, MO 65622-0436 417-345-2632	Daviess County County Courthouse 102 North Main St. Gallatin, MO 64640 660-663-2641
DeKalb County County Courthouse P.O Box 248 Maysville, MO 64469-0248 816-449-5402	Dent County County Courthouse 400 North Main St. Salem, MO 65560-1436 573-729-4144
Douglas County County Courthouse P.O Box 398 Ava, MO 65608-0398 417-683-4714	Dunklin County County Courthouse P.O Box 188 Kennett, MO 63857-0188 573-888-2796
Gasconade County County Courthouse 119 E. 1st St. Herman, MO 65041-1182 573-486-5427	Gentry County County Courthouse 200 Clay ST. Albany, MO 64402 660-726-3525
Grundy County County Courthouse 700 Main St. Trenton, MO 64683 660-359-6305	Harrison County County Courthouse P.O Box 525 Bethany, MO 64424 660-425-6424

Henry County County Courthouse 100 W. Franklin Clinton, MO 64735 660-885-6953	Hickory County County Courthouse P.O Box 3 Hermitage, MO 65668-0003 417-745-6450
Holt County County Courthouse P.O Box 437 Oregon, MO 64473 660-446-3303	Howard County Country Courthouse 1 Courthouse Square Fayette, MO 65248 660-248-3400
Howell County County Courthouse 1 Courthouse St. West Plains, MO 65775 417-256-2591	Iron County County Courthouse P.O Box 42 Ironton, MO 63650 573-546-2912
Jasper County County Courthouse 302 S. Main St. Carthage, MO 64836 417-358-0421	Johnson County County Courthouse 300 N. Holden St. Warrensburg, MO 64093 660-747-2112
Knox County County Courthouse 107 N. 4th St. Edina, MO 63537 660-397-2184	Lafayette County County Courthouse 1001 Main St. Lexington, MO 64067 660-259-4315
Lawrence County County Courthouse P.O Box 309 Mount Vernon, MO 65712-0309 417-466-3666	Lewis County County Courthouse P.O Box 67 Monticello, MO 63457-0067 573-767-5205
Lincoln County County Courthouse 201 Main St. Troy, MO 63379-1127 636-528-4415	Linn County County Courthouse P.O Box 92 Linneus, MO 64653 660-895-5417

Livingston County	Macon County
County Courthouse	County Courthouse
700 Webster	P.O Box 96
Chillicothe, MO 64601	Macon, MO 63552
660-646-2293	660-385-2913
Madison County	Maries County
County Courthouse	County Courthouse
1 Court Square	P.O Box 205
Fredericktown, MO 63645	Vienna, MO 65582
573-783-2176	573-422-3388
Marion County	McDonald County
100 South Main St.	County Courthouse
Palmyra, MO 63461	P.O Box 665
573-769-2549	Pineville, MO 64856-0665
	417-223-4717
Mercer County	Miller County
County Courthouse	County Courthouse
802 Main St.	P.O Box 12
Princeton, MO 64673	Tuscumbia, MO 65082-0012
660-748-3425	573-369-2317
Moniteau County	Monroe County
County Courthouse	County Courthouse
200 East Main St.	300 North Main St.
California, MO 65018	Paris, MO 65275-1399
573-796-4661	660-327-5106
Montgomery County	Morgan County
County Courthouse	County Courthouse
211 East 3rd St.	100 E. Newton
Montgomery City, MO 63361	Versailles, MO 65084
573-564-3357	573-378-4644
New Madrid County	Newton County
County Courthouse	County Courthouse
P.O Box 68	101 S. Main
New Madrid, MO 63869	Neosho, MO 64850
573-748-2524	417-451-8220

Noda Way County County Courthouse P.O Box 218 Maryville, MO 64468 660-582-2251	Oregon County County Courthouse P.O Box 406 Alton, MO 65606-0324 417-778-4096
Osage County County Courthouse P.O Box 826 Linn, MO 65051-0826 573-897-2139	Ozark County County Courthouse P.O Box 416 Gainesville, MO 65655-0416 417-679-3516
Pemiscot County County Courthouse 610 Ward Ave. Caruthersville, MO 63830 573-333-4203	Pettis County County Courthouse 415 South Ohio Sedalia, MO 65301-4453 660-826-5395
Pike County County Courthouse 115 West Main St. Bowling Green, Mo 63334-1665 573-324-2412	Polk County County Courthouse 102 East Broadway, RM11 Bolivar, MO 65613 417-326-4031
Pulaski County County Courthouse 301 Historic 66 East Waynesville, MO 65583 573-774-4701	Putnam County County Courthouse Room 204 Main St. Unionville, MO 63565 660-947-2674
Ralls County County Courthouse P.O Box 400 New London, MO 63459 573-985-7111	Randolph County County Courthouse 110 South Main St. Huntsville, MO 65259-1009 660-277-4717
Ray County County Courthouse 100 West Main St. Richmond, MO 64085 816-776-3184	Reynolds County County Courthouse P.O Box 10 Centerville, MO 63633 573-648-2494

Ripley County County Courthouse Courthouse Circle Doniphan, MO 63935 573-996-3215	Saline County County Courthouse 101 E. Arrow St. Marshall, MO 65340 660-886-3331
Schuyler County County Courthouse P.O Box 187 Lancaster, MO 63548-0187 660-457-3842	Scotland County County Courthouse 117 South Market St. RM 100 Memphis, MO 63555 660-465-7027
Scott County County Courthouse P.O Box 188 Benton, MO 63736 573-545-3549	Shannon County County Courthouse P.O Box 187 Eminence, MO 65466-0187 573-226-3414
Shelby County County Courthouse P.O Box 186 Shelbyville, MO 63469-0186 573-633-2181	St. Clair County County Courthouse P.O Box 525 Osceola, MO 64776-0525 417-646-2315
St. Francis County County Courthouse Courthouse Square Farmington, MO 63640 573-756-3623	Stoddard County County Courthouse P.O Box 110 Bloomfield, MO 63825 573-568-3339
Stone County County Courthouse P.O Box 45 Galena, MO 65656 417-357-6127	Sullivan County County Courthouse 109 North Main St. Milan, MO 63556 660-265-3786
Texas County County Courthouse 210 N. Grand Ave. Houston, MO 65483 417-967-2112	Vernon County County Courthouse 100 West Cherry Nevada, MO 64772 417-448-2500

Warren County County Courthouse 104 W. Booneslick Warrenton, MO 63383 636-456-3331	Wayne County County Courthouse P.O Box 48 Greenville, MO 63944 573-224-3011
Webster County County Courthouse P.O Box 529 Marshfield, MO 65706-0529	Worth County County Courthouse P.O Box 450 Grant City, MO 64456 660-564-2219
Wright County County Courthouse P.O Box 98 Hartville, MO 65667-0098 417-741-6661	

Montana

Beaverhead County 2 South Pacific St. Dillion, MT 59725-2799 406-683-5245	Big Born County 121 3rd St. Hardin, MT 59034-0908 406-665-3520
Blaine County 400 Ohio Chinook, MT 59523-0278 406-357-3250	Broadwater County 515 Broadway St. Townsend, MT 59701-9256 406-266-3405
Butte-Silver Bow County 155 West Granite St. Butte, MT 59701-9256 406-723-8262	Carter County 214 Park St. Ekalaka, MT 59324-0315
Cascade County 415 2nd Ave. Great Falls, MT 59401-2537 406-454-6810`	Chouteau County P.O Box 459 1308 Franklin Fort Benton, MT 59442-0459 406-622-5151

Custer County 1010 Main St. Miles City, MT 59301-3419 406-233-3343	Daniels County 213 Main St. Scobey, MT 59263-0247 406-487-5561
Dawson County 207 W. Bell St Glendive, MT 59330-1694 406-365-2022	Fallon County P.O Box 846 Baker, MT 59313-0846 406-778-7106
Fergus County 712 West Main St. Lewistown, MT 59457-2562 406-538-5119	Flathead County 800 South Main St. Kalispell, MT 59901-5400 406-758-5503
Gallatin County 311 West Main St. Bozeman, MT 59715-4576 406-582-3000	Garfield County P.O Box 7 Jordan, MT 59337-0007 406-557-2760
Glacier County 512 Main St. Cut Bank, MT 59427-3016 406-873-5063	Golden Valley County P.O Box 10 Ryegate, MT 59074-0010 406-568-2231
Granite County 220 N. Sansome Philipsburg, MT 59858-0925 406-569-3771	Hill County 315 4th St. Havre, MT 59501-3999 406-265-5481
Jefferson County P.O Box H, 201 Centennial Boulder, MT 59632-0249 406-225-4000	Lewis and Clark 316 North Park Ave. Helena, MT 59624-1724 406-447-8000
Liberty County 111 1st Street East Chester, MT 59522-0459 406-759-5365	Lincoln County 512 California Ave. Libby, MT 59923-1942 406-293-7781
Madison County 101 W. Wallace Virginia City, MT 59755-0278 406-843-4270	McCone County 1004 Ave. C Circle, MT 59215-0199 406-485-3500

Meagher County 15 W. Main St. White Sulphur Springs, MT 59645 406-547-3612	Mineral County 300 River St. Superior, MT 59872-0550 406-822-4541
Missoula County 200 West Broadway Missoula, MT 59802-4292 406-721-5700	Musselshell County 506 Main St. Roundup, MT 59072-2498 406-323-1104
Petroleum County P.O Box 226, 201 E. Main Winnett, MT 59087-0226 406-429-5551	Phillips County 314 S 2nd Ave West Malta, MT 59538-0360 406-654-2429
Pondera County 20 4th Ave. SW Conrad, MT 59425-2340 406-278-4010	Powder River County P.O Box 270 Broadus, MT 59317-0270 406-436-2361
Powell County 409 Missouri Ave, Deer Lodge, MT 59722-1084 406-846-3680	Prairie County P.O Box 125 Terry, MT 59349-0125 406-635-5575
Ravalli County 205 Bedford St. Box 5001 Hamilton, MT 58940-2853 406-375-6212	Richland County 201 W. Main St. Sidney, MT 59270-4087 406-482-1708
Roosevelt County 400 2nd Ave. South Wolf Point, MT 59201-1600 406-653-6200	Rosebud County P.O Box 47 Forsyth, MT 59327-0047 406-356-7318
Sanders County P.O Box 519 Thompson Falls, MT 59873-0519 406-827-4391	Sheridan County 100 W. Laurel Ave. Plentywood, MT 59254-1619 406-765-2310
Stillwater County 400 3rd Ave. North Columbus, MT 59019-0970 406-322-8000	Sweet Grass County 200 West First Ave. Bug Timber, MT 59011-0460 406-932-5152

Teton County 110 South Main St. Choteau, MT 59422-0610 406-466-2151	Toole County 226 1st Street South Shelby, MT 59474-1920 406-434-2232
Treasure County P.O Box 392 Hysham, MT 59038-0392 406-342-5547	Valley County 501 Court Square, Box 1 Glasgow, MT 59230-2405 406-228-8221
Wheatland County 201 A. Ave. NW Harlowton, MT 59036-1903 406-632-4891	Wibaux County 200 S. Wibaux Wibaux, MT 59353-0199 406-796-2481
Yellowstone County 217 N. 27TH St. Billings, MT 59107-5000 406-256-2701	

Nebraska

Adams County 500 West Fifth, RM 109 Hastings, NE 68901-7509 402-461-7107	Antelope County 501 Main St. Neligh, NE 68756 402-887-4410
Arthur County P.O Box 126 Arthur, NE 69121-0126 308-764-2203	Banner County P.O Box 67 Harrisburg, NE 69345-0067 308-436-5265
Blaine County P.O Box 136 Brewster, NE 68821-0136 308-547-2222	Boone County 222 South Fourth St. Albion, NE 68620-1247 402-395-2055
Box Butte County P.O Box 678 Alliance, NE 69301-0678 308-762-6565	Boyd County / County Courthouse P.O Box 26 Butte, NE 68722-0026 402-775-2391

Brown County 148 W 4th Ainsworth, NE 69210 402-387-2705	Buffalo County P.O Box 1270 Kearney, NE 68848-1270 308-236-1224
Burt County P.O Box 87 Tekamah, NE 68061-0087 402-374-2955	Butler County P.O Box 289 David City, NE 68632-0289 402-367-3091
Cass County 346 Main St. Plattsmouth, NE 68048-1964 402-296-9300	Cedar County P.O. Box 47 Hartington, NE 68739 402-254-7411
Chase County P.O Box 1299 Imperial, NE 69033-1299 308-882-7510	Cheyenne County P.O Box 217 Sidney, NE 69162-0217 308-254-2141
Cherry County P.O Box 120 Valentine, NE 69201-0120 402-376-2420	Colfax County 411 East 11th St. Schuyler, NE 68661 402-352-3434
Clay County 111 West Fairfield Clay Center, NE 68933-1499 402-762-3463	Dakota County P.O Box 39 Dakota City, NE 68731-0039 402-987-2130
Cuming County P.O Box 290 West Pointe, NE 68788-0290 402-372-2144	Dawson County P.O Box 370 Lexington, NE 68850-0370 308-324-2127
Dawes County 451 Main St. Chadron, NE 69337-2649 308-432-0100	Dixon County P.O Box 546 Ponca, NE 68770 402-755-2208
Deuel County P.O Box 327 Chappell, NE 69129-0327 308-874-3308	Dodge County 435 North Park Fremont, NE 68025 402-727-2767

Douglass County 1819 Farman St Omaha, NE 68102 402-444-7150	Dundy County P.O Box 506 Benkelman, NE 69021-0506 308-423-2058
Fillmore County P.O Box 307 Geneva, NE 68361-0307 402-759-4931	Franklin County County Courthouse P.O Box 146 Franklin, NE 68939-0146 308-425-6202
Frontier County P.O Box 40 Stockville, NE 69042-0040 308-367-8641	Furnas County P.O Box 387 Beaver City, NE 68926-0387 308-268-4145
Gage County P.O Box 429 Beatrice, NE 68310-0429 402-223-1300	Garden County P.O Box 486 Oshkosh, NE 69154-0486 308-772-3924
Garfield County P.O Box 218 Burwell, NE 68823-0218 308-346-4161	Gosper County P.O Box 136 Elwood, NE 68937-0136 308-785-2611
Grant County P.O Box 139 Hyannis, NE 69350-0139 308-458-2488	Greeley County P.O Box 287 Greeley, NE 68842-0287 308-428-3625
Hall County 121 South Pine St. Grand Island, NE 68801-6076 308-385-5080	Hamilton County 1111 13th St. Suite 1 Aurora, NE 68818 402-694-3443
Harlan County P.O Box 698 Alma, NE 68920-0698 308-928-2173	Hayes County P.O Box 370 Hayes Center, NE 69032 308-286-3413

Hitchcock County P.O Box 248 Trenton, NE 69044-0248 308-334-5646	Holt County P.O Box 329 O`Neill, NE 68763-0329 402-336-1762
Hooker County P.O Box 184 Mullen, NE 69152-0184 308-546-2244	Howard County P.O Box 25 Saint Paul, NE 68873-0025 308-754-4343
Jefferson County 411 Fourth St. Fairbury, NE 68352-2536 402-729-2323	Kearney County P.O Box 339 Minden, NE 68959 308-832-2723
Keith County P.O Box 149 Ogallala, NE 69153-0149 308-284-4726	Keya Paha County P.O Box 349 Spring View, NE 68778-0349 402-497-3791
Kimball County 114 East Third St. Kimball, NE 69145-1401 308-235-2241	Knox County Main St, Courthouse Square Center, NE 68724 402-288-4282
Lancaster County 555 South 10th St. Rm110 Lincoln, NE 68508 402-441-7447	Lincoln County 301 North Jeffers St. North Platte, NE 69101 308-534-4350
Loup County P.O Box 187 Taylor, NE 68879-0187 308-942-3135	Madison County 110 Clara Davis Drive Madison, NE 68748 402-454-3311
McPherson County P.O Box 122 Tryon, NE 69167-0122 308-587-2363	Merrick County P.O Box 27 Central City, NE 68826-0027 308-946-2881

Morrill County P.O Box 610 Bridgeport, NE 69336-0610 308-262-0860	Nance County 209 Esther St. Fullerton, NE 68638 308-536-2331
Nemaha County 1824 N. Street Auburn, NE 68305-2399 402-274-4213	Nuckolls County P.O Box 366 Nelson, NE 68961 402-225-4361
Otoe County 1021 Central Ave. Nebraska City, NE 68410 402-873-9500	Pawnee County P.O Box 431 Pawnee City, NE 68420-0431 402-852-2962
Perkins County P.O Box 156 Grant, NE 69140-0156 308-352-4643	Phelps County P.O Box 404 Holdrege, NE 68949-0404 308-995-4469
Pierce County 111 W. Court St. Pierce, NE 68767 402-329-4474	Platte County 2610 14th St. Columbus, NE 68601 402-563-4904
Polk County P.O Box 276 Osceola, NE 68651 402-747-5431	Red Willow County 502 Norris Ave. McCook, NE 69001 308-345-1552
Richardson County 1700 Stone St. Falls City, NE 68355 402-245-2911	Rock County 400 State St. Bassett, NE 68714 402-684-3933
Sarpy County 1210 Golden Gate Drive Papillion, NE 68046-2845 402-593-2100	Saunders County P.O Box 61 Wahoo, NE 68066 402-443-8101
Scotts Bluff County 1825 Tenth St. Gering, NE 69341-2444 308-436-6600	Seward County P.O Box 190 Seward, NE 68434-0190 402-643-2883

Sheridan County P.O Box 39 Rushville, NE 69360-0039 308-327-2633	Sherman County 6300 Street Loup City, NE 68853 308-745-1513
Sioux County P.O Box 158 Harrison, NE 69346 308-668-2443	Stanton County P.O Box 347 Stanton, NE 68779-0347 402-439-2222
Thayer County P.O Box 208 Hebron, NE 68370 402-768-6126	Thomas County 503 Main St. Thedford, NE 69166 308-645-2261
Thurston County P.O Box G Pender, NE 68047-0138 402-385-2343	Valley County 125 South 15th Ord, NE 68862 308-728-3700
Washington County 1555 Colfax St. Blair, NE 68008 402-426-6822	Wayne County P.O Box 248 Wayne, NE 68787-0248 402-375-2288
Webster County 621 North Cedar Red Cloud, NE 68970 402-746-2716	Wheeler County P.O Box 127 Bartlett, NE 68622 308-654-3235
York County 510 Lincoln Ave. York, NE 68467 402-362-7759	

New Hampshire

Belknap County 34 County Drive Laconia, NH 03246-2900 603-524-3579	Carrol County P.O Box 152 Ossipee, NH 03864-0152 603-539-2428

Cheshire County 33 West St. Keene, NH 03431-3403 603-352-8215	Coos County P.O Box 10 West Stewartstown, NH 03597 603-246-3321
Grafton County RR1, Box 67 North Haverhill, NH 03774-9758 603-787-6941	Hillsborough County 19 Temple St. Nashua, NH 03060-3472 603-627-5600
Merrimack County 163 North Main St. Concord, NH 03301 603-228-0331	Rockingham County 99-119 North Road Brentwood, NH 03833 603-679-2256
Strafford County P.O Box 799 Dover, NH 03821-0799 603-742-1458	Sullivan County 14 Main St. Newport, NH 03773-1515 603-863-2560

New Jersey

Atlantic County 5911 Main St. Mays Landing, NJ 08330 609-645-5900	Bergen County 21 Main St. Hackensack, NJ 07601 201-336-6200
Burlington County 49 Rancocas Road, PO Box 6000 Mount Holly, NJ 08060-600 609-265-5020	Camden County 520 Market St. 16th Floor Camden, NJ 08102 856-225-5354
Cape May County 4 Moore Rd Cape May, NJ 08210-1601 609-465-1065	Cumberland County 790 East Commerce St. Bridgeton, NJ 08302 856-453-2125
Essex County 465 Martin Luther King Blvd Newark, NJ 07102-1705 973-621-4492	Gloucester County 1 North Broad St. Woodbury, NJ 08096-4611 856-853-3200

Hudson County 583 Newark Ave. Jersey City, NJ 07306-1803 201-795-6200	Hunterdon County 1 East Main St, Victorian Plaza Flemington, NJ 08822 908-788-1102
Mercer County P.O Box 8068 Trenton, NJ 08650-0068 609-989-6584	Middlesex County P.O Box 871 New Brunswick, NJ 08903-0871 732-745-3000
Monmouth County P.O Box 1255 Freehold, NJ 07728-1255 732-431-7387	Morris County P.O Box 900 Morristown, NJ 07963-0900 973-285-6010
Ocean County 101 Hooper Ave. Toms River, NJ 08754-2191 732-244-2121	Salem County 92 Market St. Salem, NJ 08079-1913 856-935-7510
Somerset County P.O Box 3000 Somerville, NJ 08876-1262 908-231-7030	Sussex County County Administration Building Plotts Road Newton, NJ 07860 973-579-0210
Union County County Courthouse 2 Broad St. Elizabeth, NJ 07207 908-527-4000	Warren County County Courthouse 413 Second St. Belvidere, NJ 07823-1949 908-475-6211

New York

Albany County 112 State St. Albany, NY 12207-2005 518-447-7300	Allegany County 7 Court St. Belmont, NY 14813 716-268-7612
Broome County P.O Box 1766 Binghamton, NY 13902-1766 607-778-2109	Cattaraugus County 303 Court St. Little Valley, NY 14755-1028 716-938-9111

Cayuga County 160 Genesee St. Auburn, NY 13021-3424 315-253-1308	Chautauqua County Gerace Office Building 1 North Erie St. Mayville, NY 14757 716-753-7111
Chemung County John H. Hazlett Building 203 Lake St. Elmira, NY 14902-9588 607-737-2912	Chenango County County Office Building 5 Court St. Norwich, NY 13815 607-337-1430
Clinton County County Government Center 137 Margaret St. Plattsburgh, NY 12901-2975 518-565-4600	Columbia County County Courthouse 401 State St. Hudson, NY 12534-1915 518-828-1527
Cortland County 60 Central Ave. Cortland, NY 13045 607-753-5052	Delaware County 111 Main St. Delhi, NY 13753 607-746-6691
Dutchess County 22 Market St. Poughkeepsie, NY 12601-3222 914-486-2020	Erie County 25 Delaware Ave. Buffalo, NY 14202-3903 716-858-7500
Essex County P.O Box 217 Elizabethtown, NY 12932 518-873-3700	Franklin County 63 W. Main St. Malone, NY 12953 518-483-6767
Fulton County 223 West Main St. Johnstown, NY 12095 518-736-5555	Genesee County Main and Court Streets Batavia, NY 14020 716-344-2550
Greene County Main Bridge St. Catskill, NY 12414-0467 518-943-2050	Hamilton County P.O Box 205 Lake Pleasant, NY 12108 518-548-6651

Herkimer County 109 Mary St. Ste. 1310 Herkimer, NY 13350 315-867-1002	Jefferson County 175 Arsenal St. Watertown, NY 13601-2522 315-785-3000
Lewis County 7660 State St. Lowville, NY 13367 315-376-5355	Livingston County 6 Court St. Geneseo, NY 14454 716-243-7000
Madison County P.O Box 668 Wampsville, NY 13163-0668 315-366-2011	Monroe County 39 West Main St. Rochester, NY 14614 716-428-5301
Montgomery County P.O Box 1500 Fonda, NY 12068-1500 518-853-3431	Nassau County County Courthouse Mineola, NY 11501-4813 516-571-3000
New York City 52 Chamber St. New York City, NY 10007 212-788-3000	Niagara County County Courthouse Lockport, NY 14094-2740 716-439-7000
Oneida County 800 Park Ave. Utica, NY 13501-2939 315-798-5900	Onondaga County 407 Courthouse Syracuse, NY 13202 315-435-2070
Ontario County 27 North Main St. Canandaigua, NY 14424 716-396-4400	Orange County 255-275 Main St. Goshen, NY 10924-1621 845-291-4000
Orleans County 3 S. Main St. Courthouse Square Albion, NY 14411-1495 716-589-7053	Oswego County 46 E. Bridge St. Oswego, NY 13126 315-349-3235
Otsego County 197 Main St. Cooperstown, NY 13326-1129 607-547-4200	Putnam County 40 Gleneida Ave. Carmel, NY 10512-1798 845-225-3641

Rensselaer County 1600 7th Ave. Troy, NY 12180-3409	Rockland County 11 New Hampstead Rd New City, NY 10956-3636 845-638-5100
Saratoga County County Municipal Center 40 McMasters St. Ballston Spa, NY 12020-1986 518-885-5388	Schenectady County 620 State St. Schenectady, NY 12305-2114 518-388-4220
Schoharie County P.O Box 429 Schoharie, NY 12157-0429 518-295-8316	Schuyler County 105 Ninth St. Watkins Glen, NY 14891 607-535-8100
Seneca County 1 Dipronio Drive Waterloo, NY 13165-1680 315-539-5655	St. Lawrence County 48 Court St. Canton, NY 13617-1194 315-379-2276
Sullivan County 100 North St. Monticello, NY 12701 914-794-3000	Tiago County 56 Main St. Owego, NY 13827 607-687-0100
Tompkins County 320 North Tiago St, Ithaca, NY 14850 607-274-5434	Ulster County 244 Fair St. Box 1800 Kingston, NY 12401-0800
Warren County 1340 State Route 9 Lake George, NY 12845 518-761-6535	Washington County Upper Broadway Fort Edward, NY 12828 518-746-2210
Wayne County 26 Church St. Lyons, NY 14489 315-946-5400	Westchester County 148 Martin Ave White Mains, NY 10601-3311 914-285-2000
Wyoming County 143 North Main St. Warsaw, NY 14569 716-786-8800	Yates County 110 Court St. Penn Yan, NY 14527 315-536-5165

North Carolina

Alamance County 124 West Elm St. Graham, NC 27253-2802 336-228-1312	Alexander County 255 Liledoun Rd. Taylorsville, NC 28681-2429 828-632-9332
Alleghany County P.O Box 366 Sparta, NC 28675-0366 336-372-4179	Anson County Wadesboro, NC 28170 704-694-2796
Ashe County 150 Gov. Cir. Suite 2500 Jefferson, NC 28640-0633 336-246-1830	Avery County P.O Box 640 Newland, NC 28657-0640 828-733-8201
Beaufort County P.O Box 1027 Washington, NC 27889-1027 252-946-0079	Bertie County 108 Dundee St. Windsor, NC 27983-0530 252-794-5300
Bladen County P.O Box 1048 Elizabethtown, NC 28337-1048 910-862-6700	Brunswick County P.O Box 249 Bolivia, NC 28422-0249 910-253-2000
Buncombe County 60 Court Plaza Ashville, NC 28801-3519 828-250-4001	Burke County 200 Avery Ave. Morganton, NC 28680-0219 828-439-4340
Cabarrus County P.O Box 707 Concord, NC 28026-0707 704-788-8100	Caldwell County P.O Box 2200 Lenoir, NC 28645-2200 828-757-1111
Camden County P.O Box 190 Camden, NC 27921-0190 252-338-1919	Carteret County Courthouse Square Beaufort, NC 28516 252-728-8450

Caswell County P.O Box 98 Yanceyville, NC 27379-0098 336-694-4193	Catawba County P.O Box 389 Newton, NC 28658-0389 828-465-8200
Chatham County P.O Box 87 Pittsboro, NC 27312-0087 919-542-8200	Cherokee County 701 Peachtree St. Suite 112 Murphy, NC 28906-2900 828-837-5527
Chowan County P.O Box 1030 Edenton, NC 27932-1030 252-482-8431	Clay County P.O Box 118 Hayesville, NC 28904-0118 828-389-0089
Cleveland County P.O Box 1210 Shelby, NC 28151-1210 704-484-4800	Columbus County 111 Washington St. Whiteville, NC 28472-3323 910-642-5700
Craven County 302 Broad St. New Bern, NC 28560 252-636-6600	Cumberland County P.O Box 1829 Fayetteville, NC 28302-1829 910-678-7771
Currituck County P.O Box 39 Currituck, NC 27929-0039 252-232-2075	Dare County P.O Box 1000 Manteo, NC 27954-1000 252-473-1101
Davidson County P.O Box 1067 Lexington, NC 27293-1067 336-242-2000	Davie County 123 S. Main St. Mocksville, NC 27028-2436 336-751-5513
Duplin County P.O Box 950 Kenansville, NC 28349-0910 910-296-2100	Durham County 200 East Main St. Durham, NC 27701-3649 919-560-0000
Edgecombe County P.O Box 10 Tarboro, NC 27886-0010 252-641-7833	Forsyth County 200 North Main St. Winston Salem, NC 27101 336-727-2797

Franklin County 113 Market St. Louisburg, NC 27549 919-496-5994	Gaston County 325 North Marietta St, Gastonia, NC 28052 704-852-3100
Gates County P.O Box 148 Gatesville, NC 27938-0141 252-357-1240	Graham County P.O Box 575 Robbinsville, NC 28771-0575 828-479-7961
Granville County P.O Box 906 Oxford, NC 27565-0906 919-693-5240	Greene County 229 Kingold Blvd Snow Hill, NC 28580 252-747-3446
Guilford County P.O Box 3427 Greensboro, NC 27402-3427 336-373-3383	Halifax County P.O Box 38 Halifax, NC 27839-0038 252-583-1131
Harnett County P.O Box 759 Lillington, NC 27546-0759 910-893-7555	Haywood County 215 North Main St. Waynesville, NC 28786-3845 828-452-6625
Henderson County 100 N. King St. Hendersonville, NC 28792-5097 828-697-4808	Hertford County P.O Box 116 Winton, NC 27986-0116 252-358-7805
Hoke County Main St. Raeford, NC 28376-0266 910-875-9222	Hyde County P.O Box 188 Swan Quarter, NC 27885-0188 252-926-5711
Iredell County P.O Box 788 Statesville, NC 28687-0788 704-878-3050	Jackson County 401 Grind Staff Cove Rd. Sylva, NC 28779-2922 828-586-4055
Johnston County P.O Box 1049 Smithfield, NC 27577-1049 919-989-5100	Jones County P.O Box 266 Trenton, NC 28585-0266 252-448-7571

Lee County P.O Box 4209 Sanford, NC 27331-1968 919-718-4605	Lenoir County P.O Box 3289 Kinston, NC 28502-3289 252-523-7659
Lincoln County 115 West Main St. Lincolnton, NC 28092-2601 704-736-8473	Macon County 5 West Main St. Franklin, NC 28734-3005 828-349-2025
Madison County P.O Box 579 Marshall, NC 28753-0579 828-649-2521	Martin County P.O Box 668 Williamston, NC 27892-0668 252-792-1901
McDowell County 60 East Court St. Marion, NC 28752-4014 828-652-7121	Mecklenburg County 600 East Fourth St. Charlotte, NC 28231 704-336-2472
Mitchell County 239 Crimson Laurel Way Bakersville, NC 28705-0409 828-688-2139	Montgomery County P.O Box 425 Troy, NC 27371-0425 910-576-4211
Moore County P.O Box 905 Carthage, NC 28327-0905 910-947-6363	Nash County / County Courthouse 120 W. Washington St. Ste. 3072 Nashville, NC 27856 252-459-9800
New Hanover County 320 Chestnut St., RM 502 Wilmington, NC 28401-4027 910-341-7184	North Hampton County P.O Box 808 Jackson, NC 27845-0808 252-534-2501
Onslow County 625 Court St. Jacksonville, NC 28540 910-455-4458	Orange County P.O Box 8181 Hillsborough, NC 27278-8181 919-732-8181
Pamlico County P.O Box 776 Bayboro, NC 28515-0776 252-745-3133	Pender County P.O Box 5 Burgaw, NC 28425-0005 910-259-1200

Perquimans County P.O Box 45 Hertford, NC 27944-0045 252-426-8484	Person County 304 S. Morgan St. Rm 212 Roxboro, NC 27573-5245 336-597-1720
Pitt County 100 West Third St. Greenville, NC 27834 252-830-6300	Polk County P.O Box 308 Columbus, NC 28722-0308 828-894-3301
Randolph County 145 Worth St. Asheboro, NC 27203 336-318-6300	Richmond County P.O Box 504 Rockingham, NC 28380-0504 910-997-8200
Robeson County 701 Worth Elm St. Lumberton, NC 28358-4891 910-671-3022	Rockingham County 371 NC65, Suite 206 Wentworth, NC 27375-0206 336-342-8100
Rowan County 130 W. Innes St. Salisbury, NC 28144 704-636-0361	Rutherford County 289 N. Main St. Rutherfordton, NC 28139 828-287-6060
Sampson County 435 Rowan Rd Clinton, NC 28328-4700 910-592-6308	Scotland County P.O Box 489 Laurinburg, NC 28353-0489 910-277-2406
Stanly County 201 S. 2nd St. Albemarle, NC 28001-5747 704-983-7200	Stokes County P.O Box 20 Danbury, NC 27016-0020 336-593-2811
Surry County 118 Hamby Rd Dobson, NC 27017-8820 336-401-8201	Swain County 101 Mitchell St. Bryson City, NC 28713-2001 828-488-9273
Transylvania County 28 E. Main St. Brevard, NC 28712-3738 828-884-3162	Tyrrell County P.O Box 449 Columbia, NC 27925-0449 252-796-1371

Union County 500 N. Main St. Rm 921 Monroe, NC 28112 704-283-3810	Vance County 122 Young St. Suite B Henderson, NE 27536-4292 252-738-2120
Wake County P.O Box 550 Raleigh, NC 27602-0550 919-856-6160	Warren County P.O Box 619 Warrenton, NC 27589-0619 252-257-3115
Washington County P.O Box 1007 Plymouth, NC 27962-1007 252-793-5823	Watauga County 842 West King St. Boone, NC 28607-3525 828-265-8015
Wayne County P.O Box 227 Goldsboro, NC 27533-0227 919-731-1435	Wilkes County Courthouse Square Wilkesboro, NC 28697-2429 336-651-7300
Wilson County P.O Box 1728 Wilson, NC 27894-1728 252-399-2803	Yadkin County P.O Box 146 Yadkinville, NC 27055-0146 336-679-4200
Yancy County Room 11 Burnsville, NC 28714 828-682-3819	

North Dakota

Adams County 602 Adams Ave. Hettinger, ND 58639 701-567-2468	Barnes County 230 4th St. NW Valley City, ND 58072-2947 701-845-8500
Benson County 311 B Avenue South Minnewauken, ND 58351-0206 701-473-5340	Billings County 495 4th St. Medora, ND 58645-0168 701-623-4377

Bottineau County 314 West 5th St. Bottineau, ND 58318-1204 701-228-2225	Bowman County 104 1st St. NW Bowman, ND 58623 701-523-5421
Burke County 4001 Main St. Bowbells, ND 58721-0310 701-377-2875	Cass County 211 Ninth St. South, Box 2806 Fargo, ND 58108 701-241-5609
Cavalier County 901 3rd St. Langdon, ND 58249-2457 701-256-2229	Dickey County 309 North 2nd Ellendale, ND 58436-0215 701-349-3249
Divide County 300 Second Avenue Crosby, ND 58730-0049 701-965-6351	Dunn County P.O Box 105 Manning, ND 58642-0105 701-573-4448
Eddy County 524 Central Avenue New Rockford, ND 58356-1698 701-947-2434	Emmons County P.O Box 129 Linton, ND 58552-0129 701-254-4807
Foster County 1000 North Central Avenue Carrington, ND 58421-0104 701-652-2441	Golden Valley County 150 1st Avenue Beach, ND 58621 701-872-4331
Grand Forks County 124 South 4th St. Grand Forks, ND 58201-4782 701-780-8200	Grant County P.O Box 227 Carson, ND 58529-0227
Griggs County 808 Rollin Ave, SW Cooperstown, ND 58425 701-797-3117	Hettinger County 339 Pacific Ave. Mott, ND 58646 701-824-2515
Kidder County 120 East Broadway Steele, ND 58482 701-475-2632	Lamoure County 202 4th Ave, NE Lamoure, ND 58458 701-883-5301

Logan County 301 Broadway Napoleon, ND 58561 701-754-2425	McHenry County P.O Box 147 Towner, ND 58788-0147 701-537-5724
McIntosh County 112 NE 1st NE Ashley, ND 58413 701-288-3347	McKenzie County P.O Box 543 Watford City, ND 58854-0543 701-444-3616
Mclean County 712 5th Ave. Washburn, ND 58577 701-462-8541	Mercer County P.O Box 39 Stanton, ND 58571-0039 701-745-3292
Morton County 210 2nd Ave. NW Mandan, ND 58554-3124 701-667-3300	Mountrail County P.O Box 69 Stanley, ND 58784-0069 701-628-2145
Nelson County 210 West B Ave. P.O Box 585 Lakota, ND 58344-0585 701-247-2463	Oliver County 115 Main St. Center, ND 58530 701-794-8777
Pembina County 301 Dakota St. W Cavalier, ND 58220 701-265-4231	Pierce County 240 SE 2nd St. Rugby, ND 58368-1830 701-776-5225
Ramsey County 524 4th Ave. Devils Lake, ND 58301 701-662-7007	Ransom County P.O Box 668 Lisbon, ND 58054-0668 701-683-5823
Renville County 205 Main St. East Mohall, ND 58761 701-756-6301	Richland County 418 2nd Ave. N Wahpeton, ND 58075-4400 701-642-7700
Rolette County P.O Box 939 Rolla, ND 58367-0939 701-477-5665	Sargent County 355 Main St. Forman, ND 58032-0177 701-724-6241

Sheridan County P.O Box 636 McClusky, ND 58463-0636 701-363-2205	Sioux County 302 2nd Ave. Fort Yates, ND 58538 701-854-3481
Slope County 206 S. Main St. Amidon, ND 58620 701-879-6276	Stark County 51 3rd Street East Dickinson, ND 58601 701-264-7630
Steele County P.O Box 275 Finley, ND 58230-0275 701-524-2110	Stutsman County 511 2nd Ave. Jamestown, ND 58401 701-252-9035
Towner County 2nd Street and 4th Ave. Cando, ND 58324 701-968-4340	Trail County P.O Box 429 Hillsboro, ND 58045-0429 701-436-4458
Walsh County 600 Cooper Ave. Grafton, ND 58237 701-352-2851	Ward County P.O Box 5005 Minot, ND 58702-5005 701-857-6420
Wells County P.O Box 37 Fessenden, ND 58438-0037 701-547-3521	Williams County P.O Box 2047 Williston, ND 58802-2047 701-572-1700

Oklahoma

Alfalfa County 300 South Grand St. Cherokee, OK 73728 580-596-3158	Atoka County 200 East Court St. Atoka, OK 74525 580-889-5157
Beaver County P.O Box 338 Beaver, OK 73932-0338 480-625-4742	Beckham County P.O Box 428 Sayre, OK 73662 580-928-2457

Blaine County P.O Box 138 Watonga, OK 73772-0138 580-623-5890	Bryan County P.O Box 1789 Durant, OK 74702 580-924-2201
Caddo County P.O Box 68 Anadarko, OK 73005 405-247-6609	Canadian County P.O.Box 458 El Reno, OK 73036 405-422-2422
Carter County P.O Box 1236 Ardmore, OK 73005 580-223-5290	Cherokee County 213 W. Delaware, Rm 200 Tahlequah, OK 74464 918-456-2261
Choctaw County 300 East Duke Hugo, OK 74743-4009 580-326-3778	Cimarron County P.O Box 145 Boise City, OK 73933-0145 580-544-2251
Cleveland County 201 South Jones St. Norman, OK 73069-6046 405-366-0200	Coal County 4 North Main St. Suite 3 Coalgate, OK 74538 580-927-3122
Comanche County 315 SW 5th St Lawton, OK 73501-9026 580-353-3717	Cotton County 301 North Broadway Walters, OK 73572-1271 580-875-3026
Craig County P.O Box 397 Vinita, OK 74301-0397 918-256-7559	Creek County 317 E. Lee, Suite 100 Sapulpa, OK 74066 918-224-3529
Custer County P.O Box 300 Arapahoe, OK 73620-0300 580-323-4420	Delaware County P.O 309 Jay, OK 74346 918-253-4520
Dewey County P.O Box 368 Taloga, OK 73667-0368 580-328-5668	Ellis County P.O Box 197 Arnett, OK 73832 580-885-7301

Garfield County P.O Box 1664 Enid, OK 73702 580-237-0225	Garvin County P.O Box 167 Pauls Valley, OK 73075 405-238-3303
Grady County 326 West Choctaw St. Chickasha, OK 73018 405-224-5211	Grant County 112 Guthrie, Rm 104 Medford, OK 73759 580-395-2862
Greer County P.O Box 207 Mangum, OK 73554-0207 580-782-2307	Harmon County 114 West Hollis St. Hollis, OK 73550 580-688-3658
Harper County P.O Box 369 Buffalo, OK 73834-0369 580-735-2870	Haskell County 202 East Main St. Stigler, OK 74462-2439 918-967-8792
Hughes County 200 N. Broadway St. Suite 1 Holdenville, OK 74848-3400 405-379-6739	Jackson County 101 North Main St, 101 Altus, OK 73521-3124 580-482-2370
Jefferson County 220 North Main, Rm 101 Waurika, OK 73573 580-228-2029	Johnston County 403 W. Main Tishomingo, OK 73460 580-371-3058
Kay County P.O Box 450 201 S. Main New Kirk, OK 74647-0450 580-362-2130	King Fisher 101 South Main, Rm 3 King Fisher, OK 73750 405-375-3818
Kiowa County 316 South Main, Box 653 Hobart, OK 73651 580-726-3377	Latimer County 109 N. Central Wilburton, OK 74578 918-465-4002
Le Flore County P.O Box 607 Poteau, OK 74953-0607 918-647-3701	Lincoln County 811 Manvel Ave. Chandler, OK 74834 405-258-0080

Logan County 301 East Harrison Guthrie, OK 73044 405-282-1900	Love County 405 West Main St. Marietta, OK 73448 580-276-3059
Major County P.O Box 379 Fairview, OK 73737-0379 580-227-4520	Marshall County One Courthouse Square, Rm 101 Madill, OK 73446 580-795-3165
Mayes County P.O Box 95 Pryor, OK 74362-0095 918-825-0639	McClain County P.O Box 629 Purcell, OK 73080-0629 405-527-3117
McCurtain County P.O Box 1078 Idabel, OK 74745-1078 580-286-7428	McIntosh County P.O Box 110 Eufaula, OK 74432-0110 918-689-2452
Murray County P.O Box 240 Sulphur, OK 73086-0240 580-622-3777	Muskogee County P.O Box 2307 Muskogee, OK 74402-2307 918-682-2169
Noble County 300 Courthouse Drive 1 Perry, OK 73077-0409 580-336-2771	Nowata County 229 N. Maple St. Nowata, OK 74048-2654 918-273-0175
Okfuskee County P.O Box 108 Okemah, OK 74859 918-623-0105	Oklahoma County 320 Robert S. Kerr Ave. Rm 105 Oklahoma City, OK 73102 405-270-0082
Okmulgee County P.O Box 904 Okmulgee, OK 74447 918-756-2365	Pawnee County 500 Harrison, Rm 202 Pawnee, OK 74058 918-762-2732
Payne County P.O Box 7 Stillwater, OK 74076 405-747-8338	Pittsburgh County P.O Box 3304 McAlester, OK 74502 918-423-6865

Pontotoc County P.O Box 1425 Ada, OK 74820-1425 405-332-1425	Pottawatomie County 325 N. Broadway St. Shawnee, OK 74801-6938 405-273-4305
Pushmataha County 302 SW B St. Antlers, OK 74523 580-298-3626	Roger Mills County P.O Box 708 Cheyenne, OK 73628-0708 580-497-3330
Rogers County P.O Box 1210 Claremore, OK 74018 918-341-3965	Seminole County 110 S. Wewoka, Suite 103 Wewoka, OK 74884 405-257-2450
Sequoyah County 120 East Chickasaw Sallisaw, OK 74955 918-775-5539	Stephens County 101 South 11th St, Rm 100 Duncan, OK 73533 580-255-4193
Texas County P.O Box 197 Guymon, OK 73942-0197 580-338-7644	Tillman County P.O Box 992 Frederick, OK 73542-0992 580-335-3421
Tulsa County 500 South Denver Tulsa, OK 74013 918-596-5780	Wagoner County P.O Box 156 Wagoner, OK 74477 918-485-2142
Washington County 420 S. Johnston Ave, Rm 108 Bartlesville, OK 74003-6602 918-337-2850	Washita County P.O Box 380 Cordell, OK 73632-0380 580-832-3548
Woods County 407 Government St. Alva, OK 73717 580-327-2126	

South Dakota

Aurora County P.O Box 513 Plankinton, SD 57368 605-942-7586	Beadle County P.O Box 845 Huron, SD 57350-0845 605-352-8436
Bennett County P.O Box 460 Martin, SD 57551-0460 605-685-6969	Bon Homme County 300 West 18th Ave. Tyndall, SD 57066 605-589-4212
Brookings County 314 6th Ave. Brookings, SD 57006 605-692-6284	Brown County 25 Market St. Aberdeen, SD 57401-4293 606-626-7109
Brule County 300 South Courtland Chamberlin, SD 57325 605-734-6521	Buffalo County P.O Box 146 Gann Valley, SD 57341-0146 605-293-3217
Butte County 839 Fifth Ave. Belle Fourche, SD 57717-1719 605-892-4485	Campbell County P.O Box 37 Lake Andes, SD 57356-0490 605-487-7131
Clark County P.O Box 294 Clark, SD 57225-0294 605-532-5921	Clay County 211 West Main St. Suite 200 Vermillion, SD 57069-2039 605-677-7120
Codington County 14 First Ave. SE Watertown, SD 57201-3611 605-882-6297	Corson County P.O Box 255 McIntosh, SD 57641-0255 605-273-4229
Custer County 420 Mount Rushmore Rd Custer, SD 57730-1934 605-673-4815	Davison County 200 East 4th Ave. Mitchell, SD 57301-2631 605-995-8608

Day County 710 West First St. Webster, SD 57274-1391 605-345-3102	Deuel County P.O Box 616 Clear Lake, SD 57226-0116 605-874-2312
Dewey County Treasurer's Office Main St. P.O Box 36 Timberlake, SD 57656 605-865-3501	Douglas County County Courthouse P.O Box 159 Armour, SD 57313-0159 605-724-2423
Edmunds County P.O Box 97 Ipswich, SD 57451-0097	Fall River County 906 North River St. Hot Springs, SD 57747-1387 605-745-5130
Faulk County P.O Box 309 Faulkton, SD 57438-0309 605-598-6224	Grant County 210 East 5th Ave. Milbank, SD 57252 605-432-6711
Gregory County P.O Box 413 Burke, SD 57523-0413 605-775-2664	Haakon County P.O Box 698 Philip, SD 57567-0698 605-859-2800
Hamlin County P.O Box 237 Hayti, SD 57241-0237` 605-783-3201	Hand County 412 West First Ave. Miller, SD 57362-2182 605-853-2182
Hanson County P.O Box 67 Alexandria, SD 57311-0067 605-239-4714	Harding County P.O Box 26 Buffalo, SD 57720-0026 607-375-3313
Hughes County 104 E. Capitol Ave. Pierre, SD 57501-2563 605-773-7477	Hutchinson County 140 Euclid Rm 128 Olivet, SD 57052-0128 605-387-2835
Hyde County P.O Box 379 Highmore, SD 57345-0379 605-852-2519	Jackson County P.O Box 280 Kadoka, SD 57543-0280 605-837-2422

Jerauld County P.O Box 422 Wessington Springs, SD 57382 605-539-9301	Kingsbury County 202 2nd St. SE De Smet, SD 57231 605-854-3832
Lake County 200 East Center Madison, SD 57042-2956 605-256-7600	Lawrence County 90 Sherman St. Deadwood, SD 57732-1370 605-578-1941
Lincoln County 100 East Fifth St. Canton, SD 57013-1798 605-987-2581	Lyman County P.O Box 38 Kennebec, SD 57544-0038 605-869-2247
Marshall County P.O Box 130 Britton, SD 57430-0130 605-448-2401	McCook County P.O Box 190 Salem, SD 57058-0190 605-425-2791
McPherson County P.O Box L Leola, SD 57456-0448 605-439-3314	Meade County 1425 Sherman St. Sturgis, SD 57785-1452 605-347-2360
Mellette County P.O Box C White River, SD 57579-0703 605-259-3291	Miner County 401 N. Main St. Howard, SD 57349-0086 605-772-4671
Minnehaha County 415 N. Dakota Ave. Sioux Falls, SD 57104-2465 605-367-4206	Moody County P.O Box 152 Flandreau, SD 57028-0152 605-997-3161
Pennington County 315 St. Joseph St. Rapid City, SD 57701-2879 605-394-2171	Perkins County P.O Box 126 Bison, SD 57620-0126 605-244-5624
Potter County 201 South Exene Gettysburg, SD 57442 605-765-9408	Roberts County 411 2nd Ave. East Sisseton, SD 57262 605-698-3395

Sanborn County 604 W 6th St. P.O Box 7 Woonsocket, SD 57385-0007 605-796-4513	Shannon County 906 North River St. Hot Springs, SD 57747-1387 605-745-3996
Spink County 210 East 7th Ave. Redfield, SD 57469-1299 605-472-1825	Stanley County P.O Box 595 Fort Pierce, SD 57532-0595 605-223-2673
Sully County P.O Box 265 Onida, SD 57564-0265 605-258-2541	Todd County 200 East 3rd St. Winner, SD 57580 605-856-3727
Turner County P.O Box 370 Parker, SD 57053-0370 605-297-3153	Union County P.O Box 519 Elk Point, SD 57025-0519 605-356-2041
Walworth County P.O Box 199 Selby, SD 57472-0199 605-649-7878	Yankton County P.O Box 137 Yankton, SD 57078
Ziebach County P.O Box 68 Dupree, SD 57623-0068 605-365-5157	

West Virginia

Barbour County 8 North Main St. Philippi, WV 26416 304-457-2232	Berkeley County 126 West King St. Martinsburg, WV 25401 304-264-1923
Boone County 206 Court St. Madison, WV 25130 304-369-3925	Braxton County P.O Box 486 Sutton, WV 26601 304-765-2835

Brooke County	Cabell County
632 Main St.	750 5th Ave.
Wellsburg, WV 26070-1743	Huntington, WV 25701-2072
304-737-3661	304-526-8625
Calhoun County	Clay County
P.O Box 230	P.O Box 190
Grantsville, WV 26147-0230	Clay, WV 25043-0190
304-354-6725	304-587-4295
Doddridge County	Fayette County
118 East Court St.	P.O Box 307
West Union, WV 26456-1297	Fayetteville, WV 25840-0307
304-873-2631	304-574-4014
Gilmer County	Grant County
10 Howard St.	5 Highland Ave.
Glenville, WV 26351	Petersburg, WV 26847-1705
305-462-7641	304-257-4550
Greenbrier County	Hampshire County
P.O Box 506	P.O Box 806
Lewisburg, WV 24901-0506	Romney, WV 26757-0806
305-647-6602	304-822-5112
Hancock County	Hardy County
102 North Court St.	204 Washington St. Rm 111
New Cumberland, WV 26047	Moorefield, WV 26836
304-564-3311	305-538-2929
Harrison County	Jackson County
301 West Main St.	P.O Box 800
Clarksburg, WV 26301-2909	Ripley, WV 25271
304-624-8611	304-372-2011
Jefferson County	Kanawha County
P.O Box 250	P.O Box 3627
Charlestown, WV 25414-0250	Charleston, WV 25336
304-728-3284	305-357-0101
Lewis County	Lincoln County
P.O Box 87	P.O Box 497
Weston, WV 26452-0087	Hamlin, WV 25523
304-269-8200	304-824-7990

Logan County 300 Stratton St. Logan, WV 25601 304-792-8600	Marshall County P.O Box 459 Moundsville, WV 26041-0459 304-845-1220
Mason County 200 6th Street Point Pleasant, WV 25550 304-675-1997	McDowell County 90 Wyoming St. Ste. 111 Welch, WV 24801-2487 304-436-8544
Mingo County P.O Box 1197 Williamson, WV 25661-1197 304-235-0381	Monroe County P.O Box 350 Union, WV 24983-0350 304-772-3096
Morgan County P.O Box 28 Berkeley Springs, WV 25411 304-258-8540	Nicholas County 700 Main St. Summersville, WV 26651 304-872-7830
Ohio County 1500 Chapline St. Wheeling, WV 26003-3553 304-234-3628	Pendleton County P.O Box 187 Franklin, WV 26807 304-358-2505
Pleasants County 301 Courtlane, Suite 101 Saint Marys, WV 26170 304-684-7542	Pocahontas County 900 C 10th St. Marlinton, WV 24954-1310 304-799-4549
Preston County 101 West Main St. Kingwood, WV 26537-1198 304-329-1805	Putnam County 3389 Winfield Rd Winfield, WV 25213 304-586-0202
Raleigh County 215 Main St. Beckley, WV 25801 304-255-9146	Randolph County P.O Box 368 Elkins, WV 26241-0368 304-636-0543
Ritchie County 115 East Main St. Rm 201 Harrisville, WV 26362 304-643-2164	Roane County P.O Box 69 Spencer, WV 25276-0069 304-927-2860

Summers County P.O Box 97 Hinton, WV 25951-0066	Taylor County 214 West Main St Grafton, WV 26354 304-265-1401
Tucker County 215 1st St. Parsons, WV 26287 304-478-2866	Tyler County P.O Box 66 Middlebourne, WV 26149-0066 304-758-2102
Upshur County 38 West Main St. Buckhannon, WV 26201 304-472-1068	Wayne County P.O Box 248 Wayne, WV 25570-0248 304-272-6369
Webster County 2 Court Square, Rm G-1 Webster Springs, WV 26288 304-847-2508	Wetzel County P.O Box 156 New Martinsville, WV 26155 304-455-8224
Wirt County P.O Box 53 Elizabeth, WV 26143-0053 304-275-4271	Wood County 1 Court Square Parkersburg, WV 26101 304-424-1850
Wyoming County P.O Box 309 Pineville, WV 24874-0309 304-732-8000	

Wyoming

Albany County Grand Ave. Laramie, WY 82070 307-721-2541	Big Horn County 420 C Street Basin, WY 82410 307-568-2357
Campbell County 500 South Gillette Ave. Gillette, WY 82716-4239 307-682-7283	Carbon County P.O Box 6 Rawlins, WY 82301-0006 307-328-2668

Converse County 107 North 5th St. Suite 114 Douglas, WY 82633 307-358-2244	Crook County P.O Box 37 Sundance, WY 82729-0037 307-283-1323
Fremont County 450 North Second Rm 220 Lander, WY 82520-2337 307-332-2405	Goshen County P.O Box 160 Torrington, WY 82240-0160 307-532-4051
Hot Springs County 415 Arapahoe Thermopolis, WY 82443-2731 307-864-3515	Johnson County 76 North Main St. Buffalo, WY 82834-1847 307-684-7555
Laramie County 310 West 19th St. Suite 300 Cheyenne, WY 82001 307-633-4260	Lincoln County 925 Sage Ave. Kemmerer, WY 83101 307-877-9056
Natrona County P.O Box 863 Casper, WY 82602-0863 307-235-9202	Niobrara County 424 S. Elm, Box 420 Lusk, WY 82255-0420 307-334-2211
Park County 1002 Sheridan Ave. Cody, WY 82414-3532 307-527-8500	Platte County P.O Box 728 Wheatland, WY 82201-0728 307-322-3555
Sheridan County 244 S. Main Sheridan, WY 82801 307-674-6722	Sublette County P.O Box 250 Pinedale, WY 82941-0250 307-367-4372
Sweetwater County P.O Box 730 Green River, WY 82935-0730 307-875-9360	Teton County P.O Box 3594 Jackson, WY 83001 307-733-4430
Uinta County 225 9th St. Evanston, WY 82930 307-783-0301	Washakie County P.O Box 260 Worland, WY 82401-0260 307-347-6491

Weston County	
1 West Main St.	
Newcastle, WY 82701-2106	
307-746-2684	

About The Author

Nyene Baker is a seasoned investor and entrepreneur who has owned and operated in business for the past 13 years. He graduated from Princeton Real Estate School, and he's currently majoring in psychology. His years in business have motivated him to put this book together to help the masses take advantage of this well-kept secret

Tax Lien Certificates by Nyene Henry Baker Jr.
ORDER FORM
*Please go to **bakerinternational.org** website
to purchase online*
E-mail Order : bakerinternational1@gmail.com
Postal Order: Baker International Publishing LLC
P.O. Box 1105, Morrisville, PA 19067

Please send _copies of *Tax Lien Certificates* to:

Person or Company Ordering: _____
Address: _____
City: _____ State/Prov._____
Postal Zip Code: _____E-mail:_____
Tel #: _____Fax#:_____

No. of copies ____
Cost per copy$____ ($15.00)
Shipping $___($5 per copy)

Payment
Check __ **VISA**/Credit Card __ Money Order __

Credit Card Number : _____Exp.date __/__

Cardholder Name: _____
Cardholder signature: _____

www.ingramcontent.com/pod-product-compliance
Lightning Source LLC
LaVergne TN
LVHW051242080426
835513LV00016B/1714